RETURN
of the
REMNANT

~ PROPERTY OF ~
Darren & Julianne Patton
2242 Silver Star Drive
Banning, CA 92220
(909) 922-0877

This book is from the library of
DARREN & JULIANNE PATTON
25571 Lane Street
Loma Linda, CA 92354
(909) 796-5734

RETURN of the REMNANT

THE REBIRTH OF MESSIANIC JUDAISM

Dr. MICHAEL SCHIFFMAN

LEDERER MESSIANIC PUBLISHERS
BALTIMORE, MARYLAND

Unless otherwise noted, all Biblical quotations are based upon *The Holy Bible*, New International Version, International Bible Society. Copyright ©1973, 1978, 1984, (used by permission of Zondervan Bible Publishers) or the *Jewish New Testament*, Jewish New Testament Publications, P.O. Box 615, Clarksville, Md. 21029, Copyright ©1989,1990,1991,1994,1995 (used by permission).

Duplication of this book in full or in part, except for brief quotations, without the written permission of the publisher is in violation of the Biblical commandment and may violate Federal and State laws.

All rights reserved
Copyright ©1992, 1996 Michael H. Schiffman
ISBN 1-880226-53-7

First published as *Return From Exile: The Re-Emergence of the Messianic Congregational Movement*, ©1990.

Printed in the United States of America

Lederer Messianic Publishers
6204 Park Heights Avenue, Baltimore, MD 21215
Call 410-358-6471 for a complete catalog of Messianic products—
books, videos, tapes, CDs, Judaica, and more.
To order products call 800-410-7367 or http://www.goshen.net/lederer

DEDICATION

To my wife *Robyn*, who is the joy of my life, and my partner in Yeshua's service. She is a constant reminder of God's love and grace to me.

and

To my children, *Sara and Marcus*, because this book represents their heritage, and it is to them and to the entire generation of Messianic children emerging in our movement that I wish to pass it on.

and

To my parents, grandparents, and sisters whom I hope and pray will someday join us in the knowledge of our people's Messiah.

ACKNOWLEDGMENTS

I would like to acknowledge the following people who have greatly impacted my life, Louis Goldberg, Victor Walter, Thomas McComiskey, and Elmer and Jean Hiebert. From them I learned both academically and about serving Yeshua.

I would like to express special thanks to Elliot Klayman, who encouraged me along the way, Marcy and Chris Kotting, and Carole Abend for proof-reading this document. Their love, help and encouragement are greatly appreciated and helped make this book possible.

FOREWORD

Dr. Schiffman's book is a most significant contribution to understanding the Messianic congregational movement of God. There have been a few classical books focused on Messianic Jewish history or some other singular topic relevant to the Messianic Jewish movement. There have been some popular books which seek to define this movement of God. This book explains the existence of Messianic congregations today. It provides theological insight into the Messianic congregation in the plan of God. This is not the end of the subject but will undoubtedly spur others to contribute to the congregational mosaic, to identify and define this movement from both historical and theological perspectives. Dr. Schiffman here challenges the next authors to heightened research and scholarship.

Dr. Schiffman writes with clarity in answering a variety of *hard questions* that have arisen as a result of the recent emergence of the Messianic congregation. Who are we? Where did we come from? What are we? What is our theological basis? What is our relationship to the law, to the whole body of believers, and to the people of Israel?

The Messianic Jewish movement is a movement of restoration that has re-awakened from dormancy and re-emerged to challenge the whole body of Messiah. It is a challenge to the Jewish person who comes to the Lord just as much as it is a challenge to the believing Gentile. It challenges denominations to re-examine their theological stance on Israel and the people of God. It challenges the local church to re-examine and rediscover its origins. Dr. Schiffman writes with the perspective that this movement is of God and that it will play a pivotal role in the salvation of the people of God.

Appendix One is one of the first comprehensive surveys profiling Messianic congregations. It has a practical bent to its presentation of the statistics. It suggests what makes congregations grow. Appendices Two and Three are both useful, as well.

Dr. Schiffman has captured in his book the centrality and permanence of the Messianic congregation. It is an intricate part of the Messianic Jewish movement. Consequently, this book will be a mainstay on the shelves of those seeking to learn more about this movement.

Elliot Klayman, President
Union of Messianic Jewish Congregations
June 1990

PREFACE

"Thou shalt arise and have mercy upon Zion, for the time to favor her, yea the set time is come" (Psalm 102:13).

It is amazing and exciting to think that we are in the days to which the above verse refers. It is an undeniable fact that more has occurred in the last few years in the growth of Messianic Judaism than at any time since the first century. We are seeing congregations of Jewish believers in Jesus (Yeshua) spring up here in our own communities and around the globe. The miraculous part of it all is that it is by God's spirit, orchestrated not by programs, boards, or committees, but from above.

In his well researched book, Michael Schiffman focuses on the very heart of this Messianic awakening, this outpouring of God's spirit upon the Jewish people—the Messianic synagogue. He looks at common areas of expression and practices in this multi-faceted movement and gets to the core of what makes Messianic Judaism what it is—the most exciting resurgence of biblical religion since the resurrection of Yeshua the Messiah.

Michael Wolf, President
Messianic Jewish Alliance of America
Messianic Rabbi, Beth Messiah Congregation, Cincinnati
June 1990

TABLE OF CONTENTS

Introduction	1
Presuppositions	3
Messianic Terminology & Definitions	4
Chapter One	
Ancient Messianic History	9
Chapter Two	
Modern Messianic History	23
Chapter Three	
Messianic Congregations:	
Messiah's Message in Jewish Context	37
Chapter Four	
Messianic Synangogue or Jewish Church?	47
Chapter Five	
Messianic Jews and the Law	55
Chapter Six	
Jewish Believers and Jewish Tradition	71
Chapter Seven	
The Jewish People, the Church, and Messianic Congregations	81
Chapter Eight	
Messianic Jews and the Tri-Unity of God	93
Chapter Nine	
Messianic Judaism: a Pioneering Movement	105
Chapter Ten	
The Role of Gentiles in Messianic Congregations	113
Conclusion	121
Appendix One	
Messianic Congregation Survey Analysis	123
Appendix Two	
Participating Congregations in Opinion Survey	159
Appendix Three	
Survey of Jewish Believers in Churches	161
Appendix Four	
Messianic Trends in the 1990's	171
Bibliography	175

INTRODUCTION

Before the emergence of what is commonly referred to as the *early church,* there were Messianic congregations. The first was located in Jerusalem, led by the disciples of Yeshua. Its membership and worship style was characteristically Jewish, and from these congregations, the Good News of the Messiah went out to the peoples of the world.

In the centuries following the Nicean council of 325 C.E., Jewish believers in Yeshua lost the option of living and worshipping as Jews. They found themselves in the position of either joining existing Gentile churches renouncing their Jewish identities, recanting their faith in the Messiah to remain in the Jewish community, or maintaining their identities and faith, but not attending any worship service.

When they joined traditional Christian churches they were cut off by their family and friends, counted as having left the Jewish faith and people. They were perceived as joining the Gentiles because the churches, composed primary of Gentiles, reflected a distinctively non-Jewish culture. This change from Jewish to non-Jewish emphasis was also the result of a decidedly anti-Jewish bias in Church leadership which was manifested at the Nicean Council and thereafter in Church policies.

Many Gentiles prior to, and after the coming of the Messiah have been anti-Semitic and unfortunately some anti-Semitism continued from the Christian Church. The sad result of the millennia and a half of Christian anti-Semitism is the Jewish perception that belief in Yeshua the Messiah is both non-Jewish and anti-Semitic.

Return of the Remnant: The Rebirth of Messianic Judaism

In spite of historic anti-Semitism, the relationship between Jewish people and the Messianic faith has begun to change. Beginning in the nineteenth century, the Lord began moving upon the Jewish people and many became believers in Yeshua. According to some authorities, this constituted the largest number of Jewish believers since the first century. In the early 1970's, the Messianic Jewish movement emerged out of this earlier Jewish revival of the nineteenth century. The Messianic vision of the 1970's shared the same view of Israel's Messiah and desire for salvation of the Jewish people. What differentiated this latter development within the believing Jewish community from its earlier stages was the vision to continue living a Jewish life-style as people having accepted the Messiah. While most Jewish believers joined traditional churches, many did not. They did not see themselves as accepting something non-Jewish when they believed. They saw the Gospel and the Messiah they embraced as Jewish and as a fulfillment of God's promises to His people.

Gradually, these groups of believers began to meet regularly in home fellowships and in monthly meetings, as well as in fraternal organizations such as the Messianic Jewish Alliance. At that time there were a handful of Messianic congregations, but they were few and far between. Jewish believers meeting in Messianic congregations found they were perceived by Jewish people to be Jewish even though they believed in Yeshua. Participation in a Messianic congregation was not only a point of common cultural identity, it was a positive testimony to a skeptical, but slowly opening Jewish community.

By the late 1970's there were almost thirty congregations in North America. By the mid-1980's there were approximately one hundred. Today there are over one hundred fifty congregations. While some congregations came about as the result of the projects of mission agencies, and others through the plantings of various denominations, most have sprung up as indigenous congregations out of Bible studies and home groups. Because of their diverse beginnings, there exists a wide diversity among Messianic congregations today. Some have taken on the character of the denominations or agencies that planted them. Others have been strongly influenced by the type of Jewish community in which they are situated. Others vary because of their leader's style, education, or background. In spite of their variations, these congregations are bound together through a common Messianic vision and heritage, and a common desire to preach the Gospel to the Jew first as well as to the Gentile.

The purpose of this book is to examine the history and theology of Messianic congregations. This will bring a greater understanding of their role in the plan of God pertaining to Jewish people and Gentile believers.

PRESUPPOSITIONS

This book is based on the following presuppositions:

1. The Holy Scriptures, consisting of the Old and New Covenants, are the very word of God, are without error in whatever they seek to teach and are our only infallible rule of faith and practice (I Peter 1:21; II Timothy 3:16).

2. Yeshua (Jesus) of Nazareth is the Messiah promised to Israel, the one who fulfilled the prophecies pertaining to the first coming of the Messiah (Isaiah 53; Psalm 22; Micah 5:2; Isaiah 7:14; 9:6–7; Daniel 9:24–27; Zechariah 12:10; Deuteronomy 18:18).

3. The Gospel of Yeshua the Messiah was, is, and will be to the Jewish people first and also to the Gentiles (Romans 1:16). God has never turned away Jewish people who would turn to Him through Yeshua. It is the duty of believers in the Messiah to bring the good news of Yeshua's atoning sacrifice to the Jewish people as well as to the rest of the world.

4. There is no other way of salvation other than

through the atoning sacrifice of Yeshua. This is true for both Jewish people and Gentiles (Acts 4:12).

5. God has raised up the Messianic Jewish movement to be a witness to the Jewish people, the world in general, and to be part of His great plan of world redemption.

MESSIANIC TERMINOLOGY & DEFINITIONS

Messianic terminology is used to express the biblical faith in the Messiah because this was the culture and expression of the New Covenant faith in its earliest stages. Messianic believers wish to express their faith in the Messiah in a manner consistent with Jewish heritage and culture. This is because belief in the Messiah is consistent with being Jewish. He is the fulfillment of God's promises to Israel. Messianic terminology imparts faith in Messiah to children, friends and family in a manner consistent with Jewish heritage. It communicates biblical truth without the excess baggage of historical anti-Semitism.

The following list of terms are written and explained to assist those who are not familiar with Messianic terminology.

YESHUA: This is the name of the Messiah. *Yeshua* is a Hebrew word which has the root meaning *salvation*, as it is written, "...you shall call His name Yeshua [salvation], because He shall save His people from their sins." Transliterated into Greek as *Iesous*, it was derived into English as *Jesus*. Messianic Jews use Yeshua instead of Jesus because Yeshua is the name He was called when He walked the earth. Jewish people have been persecuted over the centuries in the name "Jesus." Consequently, that name communicates hatred and anti-Semitism. The name *Yeshua* communicates Messiah as a Jewish option for Jewish people, as well as for non-Jews.

Introduction

MESSIAH: This term is used instead of *Christ*. Messiah is derived from the Hebrew word *mashiach* meaning *anointed one*. Christ is derived from the Greek word *christos*, meaning *anointed one*. Using the Hebrew term rather than Greek emphasizes that the Messiah is for Jewish people and not exclusively for Gentiles. A second reason for using this term is, as with the name Yeshua, many thousands and perhaps millions of Jewish people have been persecuted and killed in the name of *Christ*. Christ carries a non-Jewish and anti-Jewish connotation to Jewish people.

BELIEVER: This term is used instead of the term *Christian*. To Jewish people, Christians are the people who have hated and persecuted Jews for two millennia. The word *christian* is used only three times in the New Covenant Scriptures (Acts 11:26; 26:28; I Peter 4:16). An earlier term to denote Yeshua's followers is *believers*. It is used generically of those in Messianic circles, as well as those who are in traditional churches who truly believe in Yeshua and seek to follow Him. By using the term *believer,* the focus is on a person's commitment to follow the Lord and not on the excess baggage of those who called themselves *Christians* but did not walk as He walked.

MESSIANIC: This term refers to believers involved in Messianic congregations, Jewish or Gentile. Messianic Jews are those in Messianic congregations who are of Jewish descent. Messianic refers to that expression of the biblical faith which expresses itself in a Jewish manner.

CONGREGATION: Messianic congregations are not called churches. Churches are associated with anti-Semitism by Jewish people. In the past, and

5

in some places today, anti-Semitism has come from those who profess to be believers, both from clergy and laity. *Ecclesia* refers to people not buildings. The term *congregation* does just that. A synonym in the New Covenant for *ecclesia* is *sunagoge* as it is used in James 2:1–6. There it refers to a meeting of believers. For this reason, the term congregation, or synagogue, is appropriate to describe Messianic congregations.

COVENANT: This is a reference to *testament*, meaning agreement or contract. Instead of referring to Old Testament and New Testament, Messianic believers refer to them as Older Covenant, or *Tenach* (its Hebrew name) and Newer Covenant, or *Brit Chadasha,* (Hebrew for New Covenant).

TRADITION: Jewish cultural and religious practices, whether in their original forms or adapted to reflect Messianic beliefs.

LITURGY: Jewish liturgical elements in both Hebrew and/or English which may be part of a Messianic worship service.

In addition to these terms, some Messianic believers substitute "–" for "o" in God and Lord, writing them as G–d and L–rd. This is a sign of respect in Jewish culture, just as some capitalize "G" in G–d and "L" in L–rd, even though there are no such capitalizations in the original texts of the Old and New Covenants.

Because they do not reflect our cultural expression and reflect historic anti-Semitic images, Messianic Jews do not use the following terms:

CHRISTIAN: This term was first used of non-Jewish believers in Antioch as recorded in the book of Acts. Although only used three times in the

Introduction

New Testament, it became the commonly used word to refer to Gentile believers. After the disappearance of ancient Messianic Judaism, it became the primary term used to refer to members of believing congregations. Over the centuries, the term became associated with those who hate Jewish people and reject everything Jewish. Since the term was never directly used of Jewish believers in scripture, and carries a negative historical reminder of anti-Semitism, the term *Messianic* is used. This identifies Jewish believers as followers of the Messiah, not part of the historical Christian church. (See Believer)

CONVERSION: Messianic Jews never use this term. To Jewish people conversion means turning away from being Jewish and becoming a Christian (see above). Biblically, conversion refers to repentance (i.e., turning to God). In Messianic circles, a person is spoken of as having become a believer, or becoming Messianic.

BAPTISM: Messianic Jews do not use this term either. Baptism means immersion, and the Jewish term for this is *t'vilah*. Baptism is associated with the forced conversions and baptisms perpetrated against Jewish people by anti-Semites. They did these horrible things in the name of Jesus. Baptism is considered a symbol of joining a Christian, i.e., non-Jewish, church. Messianic Jews refer to *t'vilah*, the immersion of believers, which had its origin in ancient Jewish practice. *T'vilah* means "purity." The place where *t'vilah* takes place is the *mikvah*, meaning "a gathering of waters." The act of *t'vilah* does not link Messianic Jews with any acts of anti-Semitism. The purpose of *t'vilah* is to emphasize the true Jewish roots of the faith and to separate from the people who profaned the name

7

of the Messiah by their deeds, contrary to his teaching.

CROSS: Messianic Jews do not use the symbol of the cross. To Jewish people it is a symbol of persecution in Jesus' name. Instead, they focus on its real meaning. They refer to the place where the Messiah was sacrificed as the altar or execution stake.

DATES: Dates are cited with the initials C.E. for "Common Era," or B.C.E. for "Before the Common Era." Jewish people use these initials instead of the Latin, B.C. and A.D.

This book, except for quotations, has been written in Messianic Jewish terminology and style. This gives the reader a greater understanding of Messianic cross cultural communication.

CHAPTER ONE

ANCIENT MESSIANIC HISTORY

The first Messianic congregation originated in Jerusalem, on *Shavout* (Pentecost), after the ascension of Yeshua. It carried an identifiably Jewish identity. Initially it was considered a sect of Judaism. The book of Acts records that many of the priests believed in Yeshua. It has been conjectured by a Jewish scholar that Ben Zoma, a prominent sage of the first century, was a Messianic believer.

> Suffice it to say that there are Ben Zoma references to the Last Supper, the Crucifixion and Resurrection, Christian Baptism, Original Sin and Jesus as God Incarnate in human form.

> To summarize: Ben Zoma, a Jewish sage of the Tannaitic period, who lived during the latter part of the first century and the early part of the second century, mentioned prominently in the Talmud [the codified writings of the rabbis], seems to have been attracted to Christianity and, likely, became converted to the Christian faith. His words, even when they are christological, were preserved in

the Talmudic tradition, although at times in esoteric fashion.

> From the Talmudic sources we learn that Ben Zoma was never excommunicated or even embarrassed or humiliated by his associates, the Rabbis of the period, though they took exception to and disagreed with his theological views. On the contrary, he was treated by them with sensitive consideration.[1]

When Paul arrived in Jerusalem, Jacob (James), the leader of the Jerusalem Messianic Community said, "You see brother how many tens of thousands of believers there are among the Judeans, and they are all zealots for the Torah" (Acts 21:20b). Jewish believers in Yeshua led a zealous Jewish life-style and saw their faith in Yeshua as perfectly consistent with that lifestyle. Jacob (the half-brother of Yeshua) was known as "James the Just." Hegesippus, quoted in Eusebius, recorded,

> But James the brother of the Lord, who, as there were many of this name, was surnamed the Just by all, from the days of our Lord until now, received the government of the church with the apostles....he was in the habit of entering the Temple alone and was often found upon his bended knees, and interceding for the forgiveness of the people; so that his knees became as hard as camel's, in consequence of his habitual supplication and kneeling before God. And indeed, on account of his exceeding great piety, he was called the Just.[2]

Jacob was well respected among the Jewish people of Jerusalem, but was martyred in C.E. 62. Some traditions (preserved by Josephus) blamed the Roman siege of Jerusalem as a judgment for Jacob's death.

The Messianic community in Jerusalem lived a Jewish lifestyle while trusting Yeshua as Messiah and Lord. They were never perceived by their Jewish neighbors as having embraced something non-Jewish. They were understood to be Jews who believed that their Messiah had come. While there was rivalry between Messianic Jews and the *P'rushim* (Pharisees), there was also rivalry between all the Jewish sects at that time, whether they were *Tzadukim* (Sadducees), or Essenes. Although all held to differing beliefs, there was a pluralism in the first century that allowed them to be viewed as Jews by their fellow Jews. Jacob Neusner observed,

> For this period, however, no such thing as a "normative Judaism" existed, from which one or another "heretical" group might diverge. Not only in the great center of faith, Jerusalem, do we find numerous competing groups, but throughout the country and abroad we may discern a religious tradition in the midst of great flux. It was full of vitality, but in the end without a clear and widely accepted view of what was required of each man, apart from acceptance of Mosaic revelation.[3]

It was not until after the destruction of Jerusalem in 70 C.E. that Messianic Jews were seen as being outsiders by the Jewish community. This was because of the rise of Pharisaic Judaism as the only acceptable sect of Judaism after the destruction of the Temple. All other sects were either gone or fading from the scene. This does not negate the fact that the early Jewish believers in Yeshua were still understood in their time to be Jews. Modern Jewish followers of Yeshua make the same claim to Jewish identity as their ancient counterparts for the same reasons.

The period of 66–70 C.E. was a difficult time for the whole Jewish nation. The Roman army had besieged Jerusalem since 64 C.E. The Zealot party had control of the city. Many of the religious scholars had fled the city, one being smuggled out in a coffin. It is believed that most Jewish believers left the city because of the words of Yeshua in Luke 21:20–24:

> *However, when you see Yerushalayim surrounded*

> by armies, then you are to understand that she is about to be destroyed. Those in Y'hudah must escape to the hills, those inside the city must get out, and those in the country must not enter it. For these are the days of vengeance, when everything that has been written in the Tenakh [Scriptures] will come true. What a terrible time it will be for pregnant women and nursing mothers! For there will be great distress in the Land and judgment on the people. Some will fall by the edge of the sword, others will be carried into all the countries of the [Gentiles] and Yerushalayim will be trampled down by the [Gentiles] until the age of the [Gentiles] has run its course.

Jewish believers understood this prophecy to speak of their situation, the impending destruction of Jerusalem. In obedience to the prophecy, they fled to the city of Pella in Transjordan where they settled. They continued to live a Jewish life-style and continued to see their belief in Yeshua as Jewish. Leaving Jerusalem did not repudiate their Jewish identities, nor did they turn from their Jewish life-styles. Writing in the second century, Irenaeus observed,

> They practice circumcision, persevere in the observance of those customs which are enjoined by the Law, and are so Judaic in their style of life, that they even adore Jerusalem as if it were the house of God.[4]

From this ancient Messianic community the message of Messiah went out to Jewish people in the diaspora and to the Gentiles around the world. The Messianic community had a visible presence in Jerusalem until its destruction in 70 C.E. by the Romans. When Jerusalem was besieged by the Roman armies, the Jewish believers fled to Pella where they lived in community. Eusebius records,

The whole body, however, of the church of Jerusalem, having been commanded by a divine revelation, given to men of approved piety there before the war, removed from the city and dwelt at a certain town beyond the Jordan, called Pella. Here, those that believed in Christ, having removed from Jerusalem, as if holy men had entirely abandoned the royal city itself, and the whole land of Judea;[5]

Twentieth century historian, S.G.F. Brandon believes that rather than the flight to Pella, the Messianic movement in Jerusalem was destroyed with Jerusalem. He wrote,

> Another consequence of A.D. 70, which dynamically changed the whole constitution of the church and vitally affected the future development of its organization, was the complete obliteration of the Church of Jerusalem....There can be little reasonable doubt that the sudden removal of the original source of authority made possible the emergence of other local churches, especially that of Rome, to positions of decision and control in matters of faith and practice.[6]

While it is incontestable that the influence of Messianic Judaism on the rest of the *ekklesia* was severely diminished with the destruction of Jerusalem, other factors lend credence to the Pella report. The name *meshummed* (destroyer), which rabbinic Jews have applied to Messianic Jews from early times, would make sense if they were seen as having deserted Jerusalem under siege, even if they were obeying the words of Yeshua and the oracle to flee when they saw armies surrounding Jerusalem. After 70 C.E. the Messianic community returned to Jerusalem and continued to live there until the Bar Kochba revolt against the Romans, when all Jewish inhabitants were forbidden to live in Jerusalem. Eusebius records,

> Down to the invasion of the Jews under Hadrian, there were fifteen successions of bishops in that church, all which, they say, were Hebrews from the first, and received the knowledge of Christ pure and unadulterated....For at that time the whole church under them, consisted of faithful Hebrews who continued from the time of the apostles, until the siege that took place.[7]
>
> The whole nation from that time were totally prohibited, by the decree and commands of Hadrian, from even entering the country about Jerusalem, so that they could not behold the soil of their fathers even at a distance. Such is the statement of Aristo of Pella. The city of the Jews being thus reduced to a state of abandonment for them, and totally stripped of its ancient inhabitants, and also inhabited by strangers; the Roman city which subsequently arose, changing its name, was called Elia, in honor of the emperor Aelius Hadrian; and when the church was collected there of the Gentiles, the first bishop after those of the circumcision was Marcus.[8]

In the period after Jerusalem was destroyed until the Bar Kochba revolt, Jewish people continued to live in Jerusalem. Messianic Jews returned and continued to live there until all Jews were forbidden to live there by the Roman emperor Hadrian. Eusebius recorded that the first community of Jerusalem believers which was Gentile was after this period.

In the period between 70–132, Rabbinic Judaism as we know it today had its beginning. The Jewish people no longer had the Temple in which to offer sacrifices. It was no longer possible for Jewish people to practice the biblical requirements of sacrifices and offerings. The synagogue became the center of Jewish life. Pharisaic Judaism became the norm. As the Jewish believers in Yeshua fled to Pella, the Pharisees fled to Yavneh, and in 90 C.E., under the leadership of Yochanan ben Zakkai, Judaism was reshaped into a non-sacrifice, non-Temple, religion. Without the Temple and sacrifices, Sadducean Judaism could not survive. This new form of Judaism was unacceptable to Messianic Jews because Yeshua's death is the perfect atonement for sin.

There were sharp controversies and intense rivalry between the Messianic and Rabbinic Jewish communities of this period. To the ancient prayer, the *Shemoneh Esreh,* the Eighteen Benedictions, a nineteenth was added which was actually a curse on Messianic Jews and other "sectarians." During this period, Jewish followers of Yeshua were still part of the Jewish community, living alongside other Jews.

The negative attitude of Pharisaic Judaism toward Messianic Jews was further bolstered by the defection of Jewish believers during the Bar Kochba revolt against the Romans (132–135 C.E). In the beginning, the Messianic Jews participated in the revolt. At a critical point in the war, Rabbi Akiva declared Bar Kochba to be the Messiah. While Messianic Jews could participate in a national liberation movement, they could not do so under the false messianic claims of Bar Kochba when they believed Yeshua of Nazareth was the Messiah. When, out of conviction, they withdrew from the struggle, they were branded as deserters and destroyers. In principle, they were not very different from Chasidic groups which do not recognize the modern State of Israel on the grounds that they believe it will not be legitimate until the Messiah comes. Such Chasidim are not popular for their unpatriotic stand, yet their Jewishness is not called into question. Because the Messianic Jews pulled out of the war, even though they remained intensely loyal to the Jewish state, they were ostracized by the Jewish community and considered traitors.

Messianic Judaism as a movement, along with other non-Pharisaic forms of Judaism, declined after Jerusalem was destroyed, but survived into the fourth and fifth centuries.[9] The historical development of the Church as an institution and as the sole place of salvation had overwhelming consequences for Messianic Jews as well as for the Jewish people as a whole. Because only those in the Church were saved, force and even violence could be and was often employed to coerce people to join the

Church organization "for the sake of their salvation." This often resulted in bloodshed.

Because of the drive for uniformity in the Church, Messianic Jews were seen as heretics. They worshipped in a Judaic style, maintaining their Jewish identities. However, they were not considered heretical until the Nicean period (the fourth century C.E.) because they differed from gentile believers in culture and worship forms, not theology.

The ancient name for Messianic Jews was Nazarenes. As Ray A. Pritz has said,

> The name Nazarenes was at first applied to *all* Jewish followers of Jesus. Until the name Christian became attached to Antiochian non-Jews, this meant that the name signified the entire Church, not just a sect. So also in Acts 24:5 the reference is not to a sect of Christianity but rather to the entire primitive church as a sect of Judaism. Only when the Gentile Church overtook and overshadowed the Jewish one could there be any possibility of a sectarian stigma adhering to the name Nazarene within the church itself. This should be borne in mind when considering the total absence of the name from extant Christian literature between the composition of Acts and 376 when the *panarion* [a writing of the church fathers against heresies] was written.[10]

Jewish believers were forced to either conform to the growing, larger Gentile oriented Church or be quenched as a movement. The problem was not simply one of larger numbers for the Gentile Church, but was partly a problem of the fact that the Gentile Church stressed uniformity within its ranks. As it grew as an organization, developing far beyond its biblical roots, the Jewish believers seemed more different than ever. The problem was not simply a matter of not fitting into the Gentile Church's corporate structure. Part of the problem was Gentile arrogance which Paul warned against in Romans 11:17–22.

> But if some of the branches were broken off, and you—a wild olive—were grafted in among them and have become equal sharers in the rich root of the olive tree, then don't boast as if you were better than the branches! However, if you do boast, remember that you are not supporting the root, but the root is supporting you. So you will say, Branches were broken off so that I might be grafted in. True, but so what? They were broken off because of their lack of trust. However, you keep your place only because of your trust. So don't be arrogant; on the contrary, be terrified! For if God did not spare the natural branches, he certainly won't spare you!

Historian David Rausch has observed,

> The Gentile Church claimed to be the true Israel and tried to disassociate itself from the Jewish people early in its history.[11]

This anti-Jewish sentiment which sought to separate Christianity from its Jewish roots can be seen in Chrysostom's Sermon IV. Not only did it seek to separate Christianity from its Jewish origins, making it something totally "other" than Judaism, but it sought to separate Jewish believers from their Jewish heritage.

> Let me, too, now say this against these Judaizing Christians. If you judge that Judaism is the true religion, why are you causing trouble to the church? But if Christianity is the true faith, as it really is, stay in it and follow it. Tell me this. Do you share with us the mysteries, do you worship Christ as a Christian, do you ask him for blessings, and you then celebrate the festival with his foes? With what purpose, then, do you come to the church?[12]

Apart from the Nazarene groups of this period, there were so called 'Jewish Christian' sects that were heretical. They were rightly opposed on account of their false teachings. The *Patristic literature,* the writings of the church fathers, devote more time to the heretical Jewish Christian sects than the orthodox. Perhaps it was because they were heretical, particularly the Ebionites and Elkesaites who denied the virgin birth and rejected Paul's writings and parts of the Old Testament canon.[13] These heretical groups should not have been lumped together with Nazarene Jewish believers who were scripturally sound. Klijn and Reinink observed,

> The only writers who knew something about the Nazarenes were Epiphanius and Jerome....[The Nazarenes] living in Berea and speaking Aramaic...adhered to Judaism but accepted the orthodox beliefs about Jesus and acknowledged Paul and the Gentile Christian Church.[14]

Theologically orthodox Jewish believers were confused with the heretical Ebionites and Elkesaites in the patristic literature, particularly by Epiphanius. This lumping together of the orthodox Jewish believers with the heretics reflects a patristic view that to live Jewishly as a believer was in itself heretical. Jean Danielou has written,

> The term *Jewish Christianity*...has three possible references. First, it may designate those Jews who acknowledged Christ as a prophet or a Messiah, but not as the Son of God, and thus form a separate class, half way between Jews and Christians. The second possible reference for the term *Jewish Christianity* is the Christian community of Jerusalem, dominated by James and the tendencies for which he stood. *This community was perfectly orthodox in its Christianity but remained attached to certain Jewish ways of life,* without however, imposing them on proselytes from paganism.

Finally, a third possible reference of the term *Jewish Christianity* is a type of Christian thought expressing itself in forms borrowed from Judaism.[15]

Danielou uses the third possible reference for Jewish Christianity. He encompasses gnostics and heretical groups of many different ilks, including those who had some type of emphasis rooted in Jewish thought, even if their ethnic background was not Jewish. This very broad definition included orthodox Jewish believers by reason of their identification with things that are Jewish. In following this definition, Danielou is apparently following the same definition as the Church fathers. This lack of differentiation branded orthodox Jewish believers of the second definition as heretics by reason of Jewishness, apart from any consideration of doctrine. In a similar way, the sixteenth-century Anabaptist groups were lumped together with anarchist heterodox groups and condemned by other reformers and Catholics alike.

Since the Church fathers did acknowledge the orthodoxy of the Nazarenes, forces for unity, focused on the formal Church structure developing at the time, may have been a motivating force to discourage the Nazarenes.[16] Jacob Jocz has written concerning the decline of early Messianic Judaism,

> Hemmed in between the Catholic Church and Catholic Judaism, Jewish Christianity slowly dwindled away....Its actual existence reached into the fourth and fifth centuries, especially in Syria. But it exerted no important influence either upon the Synagogue or the Church.[17]

Ray Pritz holds the view that Jewish believers were not simply hemmed in on both sides as Jocz claims, but in fact rejected the Gentile Church and Pharisaic Judaism. The significance of this view is that while Jocz's view may be accurate from a political standpoint, Messianic Jews were not helpless victims caught between two larger groups with opposing agendas. They took a bold stand for their convictions, suffering martyrdom as a

19

movement rather than being overtaken by one side or the other. He has said,

> The rejection was not solely from the Jewish side. The Nazarenes refused to accept the authority established by the Pharisaic camp after the destruction of Jerusalem, and in so refusing they adjudicated their own isolation from the converging flow we call Judaism. Just as they rejected the Church's setting aside of the Law of Moses, so they refused the rabbis' expansive interpretations of it.
>
> They never relinquished hope that Jews would one day turn away from tradition and towards Jesus: *O Sons of Israel, who deny the Son of God with such hurtful resolution, return to Him and to his apostles.*[18]

Considering themselves the true heirs to Biblical Judaism, Messianic Jews stood their ground against both Pharisaic Judaism and Hellenistic Gentile Christianity. While they existed throughout the time of Jerome, and into the early fifth century, Jewish believers thereafter had little alternative but to enter the Gentile Christian Church. In a sense, the Jewish way to follow Yeshua went into exile, not to return until the late nineteenth and early twentieth centuries when a greater climate of plurality and tolerance emerged in both the Jewish and Christian communities.

Endnotes

[1] Samson H. Levey, "Best Kept Secret of the Rabbinic Tradition," *Judaism* 21 (Fall 1972), p. 469.
[2] Eusebius, *Ecclesiastical History,* Book II, Chapter XXIII.
[3] Jacob Neusner, *First Century Judaism in Crisis* (New York: Abingdon Press, 1975), p.39.
[4] Ante-Nicean Fathers, Eerdmans, Volume I. Irenaeus, *Against Heresies. I, 26,2.*

[5] Isaac Boyle, trans. *The Ecclesiastical History of Eusebius Pamphilus* (Grand Rapids: Guardian Press, 1955), p.86.
[6] S.G.F. Brandon, *The Fall of Jerusalem and the Christian Church* (London: S.P.C.K., 1951), p.250.
[7] Eusebius, *Ecclesiastical History*, Book IV, Chapter V.
[8] Ibid., Chapter VI.
[9] Jacob Jocz, *The Jewish People and Jesus Christ*, 3rd ed. (Grand Rapids: Baker Book House, 1979), p. 199.
[10] Ray A. Pritz, *Nazarene Jewish Christianity* (Leiden: E.J. Brill, 1988), p.15.
[11] David Rausch, *Messianic Judaism: Its History, Theology, and Polity* (Lewiston, New York: Edwin Mellen Press, 1982), p.13.
[12] John Chrysostom, *Sermon Against Judaizing Christians*, Sermon IV,IV,1.
[13] A.F.J. Klijn and G.J. Reinink, *Patristic Evidence for Jewish-Christian Sects* (Leiden: E. J. Brill, 1973), pp.19–43, 54–66.
[14] Ibid., p. 52.
[15] Jean Danielou, *The Theology of Jewish Christianity* Trans. & Ed. by John A. Baker (Philadelphia: Westminster Press, 1964), pp. 7–9.
[16] S.G.F. Brandon, in *The Fall of Jerusalem and the Christian Church*, contends that the most harmful blow to the first century Messianic Jews was the destruction of Jerusalem, because the Jerusalem Messianic community lost its center as well as its most visible leadership. As the Messianic Jews scattered to their various locations, some went into heresy, others were isolated and cut off, or merged with gnosticism. This situation, combined with opposition because of developments in the Gentile wing of the church, resulted in the eventual end to the ancient Messianic movement.
[17] Jocz, *The Jewish People and Jesus Christ*, p. 199.
[18] Pritz, *Nazarene Jewish Christianity*, p.110.

CHAPTER TWO

MODERN MESSIANIC HISTORY

To Jewish believers of the first century, faith in the Messiah was a natural part of their Jewish identity. Their Messianic faith in no way nullified their Jewishness. This was the case with Jewish believers living in Jerusalem whom, we are told throughout Acts, were zealous for the Torah and worshipped in the Temple. This was also the case of Saul of Tarsus, the Apostle to the Gentiles. Paul said, *I am an Israelite myself, a descendant of Abraham of the tribe of Benjamin* (Romans 11:1b).

Jewishness is defined biblically as being a physical, lineal descendent of Abraham, Isaac and Jacob (Genesis 17:7,19; 28:13–15). Jewish identity is not mainly an issue of faith, but lineage and heritage. During the period of the kings of Israel and Judah, when the people worshiped the *Ashtarot* and *Baalim*, as well as other pagan deities, they were still called the children of Israel. Jewishness was a matter of birth, *not* faith.

In modern times, Jewishness has been defined both by lineage as well as religious affiliation. Proselytes to traditional Rabbinic Judaism are reckoned as Jews by traditional Judaism, even though they are not physical descendants. Messianic Jews are physical descendants of the patriarchs, being Jewish by birth, but are not adherents to the authority of rabbinic tradition. For this reason, the rabbinic leaders have claimed that Messianic Jews are not Jews because they believe in Yeshua as the Messiah. They claim Messianic Jews embrace a foreign god and turn from the God of

23

their fathers. Messianic Jews are not leaving the God of their fathers to follow a foreign deity. They are affirming their faith in the God of Abraham, Isaac and Jacob, recognizing Yeshua of Nazareth to be the fulfillment of God's promise to send the Messiah. This is not a turning away from the God of Israel. It is an affirmation that His promises are trustworthy.

In the period following the Nicean council in 325 A.D., Jewish believers in Yeshua were expected to renounce all things Jewish when they became believers.[1] The policy of renunciation deepened the separation between Jewish believers and the Jewish community. This historical wedge still exists in the minds of many people today, both Jewish and non-Jewish. It is also tied to a cultural Jewish self-definition which is inconsistent with the religious Jewish definition. Charles Silberman has written,

> The belief that converts to Christianity remain Jews is far more than an expression of distaste for social climbers; it is an inescapable by-product of the way Judaism defines itself—has always defined itself. The fact that there is no way to stop being Jewish is the largest, and certainly the most puzzling, difference between Judaism and Christianity. In the Jewish self-definition, belief and practice determine whether one is a *good* Jew or a *bad* Jew but not whether one *is* a Jew; to be a Jew is an indelible status, from which there is no exit.[2]

Jewish leaders are not in agreement today on who is a Jew. Traditional Jewish *halakha*[3] says that the child of a Jewish mother is Jewish. Others have added, an 'if' to the definition, requiring that the child of a Jewish mother must not have converted to another religion. Messianic Jews believe that accepting the Messiah of Israel is not accepting another religion; rather, it is returning to the promises of God to the patriarchs. Moreover, Messianic Jews use a biblical definition of Jewishness, based on ancestry. Anyone born of Jewish parents is Jewish, whether descended matrilineally or patrilineally. Messianic Jews do not see faith in the Messiah as a repudiation of their Jewishness, but a fulfillment. The Messianic Jewish claim to Jewishness is one of birthright, not rabbinic acceptance. Belief in Yeshua as the Messiah is not the adoption of a foreign deity, but belief in the promised Anointed One who came according to prophecy found in the Jewish Scriptures. For Messianic Jews, faith in Yeshua is as much a natural part of their Jewishness as it was for Jewish believers of the first centuries.

Since the fifth century, it has not been possible for Jewish believers to live in Messianic community or to practice Messianic congregational worship. Pressures from both the Jewish community and the Church squeezed out Messianic Judaism as a viable option. The Jewish community said that if you want to be a Jew, you can't believe in Jesus. The Church said that if you want Jesus, you must renounce all things Jewish. Chapter three deals with this topic in greater detail. The history of Messianic Judaism between the fifth and nineteenth centuries becomes the history of individual Jewish believers who, for the most part, became part of the traditional churches.

Because of the intolerance of the times, Jewish believers could not meet as Jewish believers, and consequently, Messianic Judaism had no formal history during this period. This lack of formal history does not negate the validity of Messianic Judaism. There were Jewish people in every century who were able to look beyond the intolerance of the times, and see that Yeshua of Nazareth is the Messiah of Israel. In his book on Hebrew Christianity, Arnold Fruchtenbaum records the period of 135 to 1800, as one brief history, because there was very little organizationally in existence at that time.[4]

Hugh Schonfield, in his book, *The History of Jewish Christianity,* said,

> The history of Jewish Christianity from the seventh century to the present day is...a record of individual converts, who, such was the intolerance of the times, scarcely dared acknowledge their Jewish extraction for fear of persecution on the ground of sympathy towards their former co-religionists.[5]

25

The re-birth of the Messianic Jewish movement is evidence that while Messianic Judaism was in a dormant period, it was not dead. As a tree begins to sprout leaves in spring, so has this movement come into spring.

The modern phenomenon of Messianic Judaism's rebirth is an important issue for Jewish believers in Yeshua. Questions of its authenticity are raised because, as a movement, it had been dormant for at least fourteen centuries. To be sure, there have always been Jewish believers in Yeshua during those centuries, among them Johann Neander, Benjamin Disraeli, Franz Delitzsch, and Alfred Edersheim.[6] Jewish believers had traditionally been part of the Gentile oriented local churches. Just as the Jewish people had been scattered throughout the nations of the world, so were Jewish believers scattered among the Gentiles in traditional churches during this same time period.

During the nineteenth century an awakening began among the Jewish people, both physically and spiritually. The Hebrew Christian Alliance of Great Britain, founded in 1866, stated in their constitution,

> Let us not sacrifice our identity. When we profess Christ, we do not cease to be Jews; Paul, after his conversion, did not cease to be a Jew; not only Saul was, but even Paul remained, a Hebrew of the Hebrews. We cannot and will not forget the land of our fathers, and it is our desire to cherish feelings of patriotism....As Hebrews, as Christians, we feel tied together; and as Hebrew Christians, we desire to be allied more closely to one another.[7]

During this same period, the Zionist movement began to take shape. The first Zionist Congress was called by Theodore Herzl in 1897 in Bazel, Switzerland, where people congregated whose dream it was to see the restoration of a free, independent Jewish state. As God had begun calling Jewish people out of the lands of dispersion, so He also began calling Jewish believers out of the spiritual dispersion in non-Jewish churches. This is a common view within the Messianic movement.

The first Hebrew Christian Alliance was founded in Great Britain on May 14, 1866. The American Hebrew Christian Alliance was founded in 1915. In 1925, the International Hebrew Christian Alliance was formed. Prior to World War II, a few Hebrew Christian congregations had been established in Europe as well as the United States: among them, the first Messianic Synagogue in Bessarabia. Schonfield records,

> It remained for Joseph Rabinowitz in 1882 to found the first Jewish Christian communion in modern times which belonged to no definite denomination, but was rather in the nature of a synagogue of Jewish believers in Jesus.
>
> His youth was spent in Hasidic circles, and he showed great promise of literary ability. When a wave of persecution broke out, he went to Palestine on a mission of inquiry with a view to establish a Jewish colony there. The Hebrew New Testament given to him many years before went with him as a guide book. When he reached Jerusalem and saw the miserable state of the Jewish inhabitants, he was deeply depressed; but before he left the Holy City he ascended the Mount of Olives. Sitting there and viewing the Mosque of Omar, where formerly the Temple stood, his mind went back over the tragic history of his people. What was the meaning of...Israel's suffering? In a flash the answer came to him: *The key to the Holy Land is in the hands of our brother Yeshua.* Rabinowitz returned to Kischineff, and with great power and enthusiasm set forth his belief. In a short time he had gathered around him numerous adherents to his doctrine no only in Kischineff, but in many other towns of Bessarabia.[8]

Rabinowitz's work was different in its Jewish expression, but also in that it was not tied to any denomination. Eric Gabe, a member of the Kischineff Messianic community, in later years wrote,

> Rabinowitz continued to observe, even as a Hebrew Christian, a number of Old Testament commandments, such as the Sabbath, circumcision and the Passover. He thus became the founder of the Hebrew Christian movement in Bessarabia, which he called "The Community of Messianic Jews, Sons of the New Covenant," in Hebrew, *Yehudim Meshichiim Bney Brit Hachadashah*.[9]

Rabinowitz was a century before his time, forming, perhaps, the first Messianic synagogue in the modern sense of that term. The terminology he used to describe himself and his congregation were clearly Messianic as would be practiced today. In his article, Gabe quotes from the book, *The Christian Movement among the Jews of Kishineff,* by I.N. Axelrad, a Jewish believer, who quotes Rabinowitz describing his work. He said,

> My spiritual work was not influenced by a church or denomination, nor did it come about by human help, but only through the goodness and great mercy of God. He revealed to me that the Synagogue and contemporary Judaism are unable to help our Jewish people....From the very outset it was my heart's desire to bring together my people and the words of the Messiah, which are spirit and life, in order that they might...recognize Yeshua as Messiah and Son of the Living God.

> In order to achieve this end, they would have to be led from a merely traditional Synagogal atmosphere to the...Holy Scriptures by an organization that would be neither Synagogue nor Church. Hence it was of great consequence to our movement that the Russian government allowed me to form a *Community of Messianic Jews, Sons of the*

> *New Covenant*...and to build an edifice specifically for the worship of God.[10]

Gabe, in another issue, describes a photograph of Rabinowitz's Messianic sanctuary. He said,

> The House of Prayer...approximated...the appearance of a Synagogue rather than that of a Church. In the photograph, Rabinowitz stands in the pulpit holding a complete copy of the Bible in Hebrew. Behind him hangs a *menorah*...just as in any Synagogue....The photograph shows some of the Hebrew texts displayed in his House of Prayer. The text on his left contains the Hebrew name of Jesus, namely YESHUA.... Separated on the right...[is] the *Aron Kodesh*— The Holy Ark—within which the sacred scrolls of the Bible are kept.[11]

It is clear from this description, that Rabinowitz was not like his contemporaries in the Hebrew Christian movement of the turn of the century, but was more like the Messianic Jews of the latter 20th century. Yet Rabinowitz was not alone. In 1898, there was a Hebrew Christian congregation in London associated with the Mildmay Mission to the Jews. In his 1902 book, *A Century of Jewish Missions,* A.E. Thompson writes of congregations of Jewish believers. Although his terminology reflects the traditional non-Messianic expression of his day, his descriptions are significant in regard to the dawning of the Messianic congregational movement. He said,

> Very noteworthy among the organizations in this field are the various Hebrew Christian assemblies that have formed. These are congregations of converts to Christianity, united for the two-fold purpose of edification and testimony. They generally adhere to the keeping of the ceremonial law, while they hold that salvation is only and altogether by

grace. A number of small congregations have existed in Europe, England and America.[12]

Thompson went on to give a description of these assemblies of Jewish believers in Jesus. He said,

> The Hebrew-Christian Assembly is an association or congregation of converts, formed in 1898 for mutual edification and for testimony to their brethren according to the flesh. The Assembly meets for worship every Sunday morning in the Mildmay Mission Building, London, and holds open air meetings for Jews in Whitechapel and Soho. The oversight of the Assembly is entrusted to an elective committee, or council. This is one of the few distinctively Jewish-Christian congregations which has seemed to prosper and its ultimate standing can not be assured at so early a date in its existence.[13]

Thompson also mentions a congregation in Smyrna:

> A Jewish Christian congregation was formed in 1894 by Abram Levi, who had been converted while lying in the Scotch Mission Hospital. The original number of heads of families in this church was sixty-four, but half of them soon withdrew on account of persecution. The remainder, like the ancient Smyrnaote church, which received the L—rd's approval, stood true. They reject the Talmud and rabbinical traditions, accept the New Testament, and retain circumcision as a national rite.[14]

In addition to these and other congregations which served as forerunners of modern Messianic Jewish congregations, the vision for such congregations existed in the mid-nineteenth century. Thompson records,

In 1867 a Jewish Christian Brotherhood was formed in New York, with a branch in Chicago....Rev. C. Lucky was sent as missionary to Galatia. He and Lowen published a periodical, "Eduth le Israel," which strongly advocated the establishment of a Jewish-Christian Church. Friedlander published another paper, "The Peculiar People," in the same interest.[15]

The significance of this brotherhood, and the subsequent congregations, is that it demonstrates that the vision for congregations of Jewish believers in the Messiah was emerging in the last century, and budded in the first half of the twentieth century.

In 1905, a Hebrew Christian congregation was established in Baltimore, Maryland under the auspices of the Presbyterian Church. The congregation still exists today, as Emmanuel Messianic Congregation. Its worship style may have changed over the years, but its vision to see Jewish people know Yeshua and worship together as Jews has remained.

In the 1930's, a congregation of Jewish believers was established in Chicago. This congregation still exists as Adat Hatikvah. It too was founded under the auspices of the Presbyterian Church.

In the 1940's and 50's, Lawrence Duff-Forbes had a Messianic Congregation in Los Angeles. He utilized Messianic terminology, had Shabbat and Jewish Holy Day services, and utilized Jewish liturgical forms in worship. He worked closely with Edward Brotzky who had a similar work in Philadelphia and later served in Toronto.

By the 1950's a Presbyterian denomination had planted four such congregations: the aforementioned Adat HaTikvah in Chicago, Emmanuel in Baltimore, as well as Beth Messiah in Philadelphia, which exists to this day. A fourth congregation was started in Los Angeles but is no longer in existence.

While some of these earlier congregations would not have been called "Messianic" in the modern sense of term, they were very much the ancestors of present day Messianic congregations.

31

The unifying factor in what constitutes a Messianic congregation is not terminology or praxis, because these factors vary from congregation to congregation. In Israel, the equivalents of American Messianic congregations vary widely in areas of tradition and practice. Their unifying factor is that they are Hebrew-speaking congregations that believe in Yeshua. This is reflective of how Israelis express identity. American Jews express Jewish identity around culture, tradition, membership in Jewish organizations, or identification with Jewish causes. In Israel, Jewish identity is expressed by living in the land and assimilating into Israeli society, which is exemplified by speaking Hebrew. The Jewish believing congregations of the last century may not have expressed themselves in modern Messianic terms, but they spoke Yiddish and celebrated Jewish Holy Days to some extent. The unifying factor was that all these assemblies, from ancient to modern, from those in the dispersion to those in Israel, were congregations of Jewish believers, meeting together as Jewish people and lifting up the Messiah.

Gabe also mentioned that after Rabinowitz's death, his work continued in the existence of the Hebrew Christian Alliance of Bessarabia, as well as in the Hebrew Christian community itself in Bessarabia. Gabe was part of that community between 1935 and 1939. The Hebrew Christian Alliance of Bessarabia, along with the others of eastern Europe were destroyed by the Nazis in the second world war. The last meeting of the Hebrew Christian Alliance of Germany held in Berlin in 1934 had over 400 in attendance.[16] The Holocaust devastated the Jewish people. This was no different for the Jewish believers. Many European Hebrew Christian alliances and congregations perished. Yet, as the State of Israel emerged from the ashes of the Holocaust, so did the Messianic movement further emerge at this time.

After the 1967 Six Day War, Jerusalem was restored to the Jewish people, fulfilling the two thousand year old prayer of the Jewish people, *Next year in Jerusalem*. From 1967 to the present day there has been a large number of Jewish people who have come to faith in Yeshua as Messiah. Together with the large number of Jewish people who came to Yeshua in the nineteenth century, when modern Zionism was born, they constitute the largest number of Jewish people to come to the Messiah since the first century. The physical phenomenon has its spiritual counterpart in Messianic Judaism. In this period, Jewish believers have not just come to Yeshua, but many have formed Messianic Jewish congregations where they worship Yeshua in a Jewish manner rather than join non-Jewish oriented congregations.

In the 1970's many other Messianic congregations formed. Today there are approximately one hundred fifty Messianic congregations worldwide. There are currently three organizations tying the congregations together: the Union of Messianic Jewish Congregations (UMJC), the Fellowship of Messianic Congregations (FMC), and the International Alliance of Messianic Congregations and Synagogues (IAMCS), the latter being tied to the Messianic Jewish Alliance of America.

The modern Messianic movement in the early stages was not known as Messianic Jewish but as Hebrew Christian. The point of view represented by the respective names was the object of sharp divisions in the movement, some of which exists to this day. David Rausch, in his book on Messianic Judaism, goes into some detail on these issues.[17] Dr. Robert Winer has observed,

> The name change [from Hebrew Christian to Messianic Jewish] was a reflection of a deeper change that had occurred, not just in the Alliance, but in Jewish followers of Yeshua all across the world. There was a sudden pull back to an almost strident Jewish identity. The crest of the long-awaited Jewish revival had the words Messianic Judaism emblazoned on it, and everyone riding that crest seemed to have caught the same vision.[18]

Messianic Judaism has emerged out of its Hebrew Christian beginnings and is its rightful descendant and heir. Differing views from within do not devalue the Messianic movement any more than the fact that some Hasidic Jewish sects opposing the formation of the State of Israel did not negate the significance of the Zionist movement.

Some would say that modern Messianic Jews are different from their Hebrew Christian predecessors. It is true they differ in respect to affiliations with churches and personal life-styles. Messianic Jews have not assimilated into churches and their non-Jewish culture. They have continued in Jewish culture and practice. Yet, it is also true that all are Jewish believers. The term *Hebrew Christian* in Hebrew is Messianic Jew, *Yehudim Meshikhim*. On the inside, they are one people.

In a greater sense, the modern Messianic movement grew out of the older Hebrew Christian movement. Hebrew Christians are the ancestors of all Jewish believers. The modern American Messianic Jewish organizations, the UMJC, FMC, or MJAA, all trace their ancestry back to the earlier Hebrew Christian alliances.

In spite of the many Messianic congregations that have come into existence, more Jewish believers are in churches than in Messianic congregations. Some people have suggested that this calls the validity of Messianic congregations into question. The presence of Jewish believers in churches no more calls Messianic Judaism's validity into question than Jewish people living outside the Land of Israel calls the State of Israel's validity into question. On the contrary, it further shows the parallel between the physical scattering and the spiritual dispersion. God's hand is on one as surely as it is on the other; it remains to be seen what God will accomplish as He brings his plan to completion.

The question posed by the existence of Messianic congregations is not whether or not they are of God. Their fruit attests to God's hand on their existence. Rather, people are faced with the question of how they will relate to this re-emerging movement, to consider to what extent they want to be part of it.

Endnotes

1. Hugh Schonfield, *History of Jewish Christianity* (London: Duckworth, 1936), pp. 108–112.
2. Charles E. Silberman, *A Certain People* (New York: Summit Books, 1985), p. 70.
3. Heb. lit. *"the way to walk."* Halakha refers to the proper way to practice Judaism.
4. Arnold Fruchtenbaum, *Hebrew Christianity: Its Theology, History, and Philosophy* (San Antonio: Ariel Press, 1983), pp. 43–48.
5. Hugh Schonfield, *The History of Jewish Christianity*, chapter 10, section 1.
6. Hugh Schonfield, *The History of Jewish Christianity,* records a historical account of Jewish believers through the centuries until the early 1930's.
7. Hebrew Christian Alliance of Great Britain, 1866, quoted in Schonfield, *The History of Jewish Christianity,* p. 222.
8. Hugh Schonfield, *The History of Jewish Christianity,* p. 225.
9. The Revd. Eric S. Gabe, "The Hebrew Christian Movement in Kishineff," published in *The Hebrew Christian*, The Quarterly Organ of the International Messianic Jewish (Hebrew Christian) Alliance, No. 3, Vol. LX, p. 87.
10. Ibid., p. 88.
11. Ibid., p. 88–89.
12. A.E. Thompson, *A Century of Jewish Missions* (New York: Fleming H. Revell Company, 1902), p. 84.
13. Ibid., pp.112–113.
14. Ibid., p. 193.
15. Ibid., p. 193.
16. from personal interview with Rev. David Sedaca, Secretary of the Americas, International Hebrew Christian Alliance, August 9, 1987.
17. David Rausch, *Messianic Judaism: Its History, Theology, and Polity*, chapters 3, 5, & 6.
18. Dr. Robert Winor, "Others Have Labored Before You," in *The Messianic Post,* MJAA, Wynnewood, Penn., April 1990, Vol. I.2.

CHAPTER THREE

MESSIANIC CONGREGATIONS: MESSIAH'S MESSAGE IN JEWISH CONTEXT

An important question that needs to be addressed at this point is, *What exactly* is *a Messianic congregation?*

Defining the term "Messianic congregation" can be complicated. A Messianic congregation may refer to various entities. The Fellowship of Messianic Congregations define a Messianic congregation as,

> A local assembly planned by the Father, united in Messiah Yeshua, and called by the Holy Spirit to organize for the purposes of worship, instruction, fellowship, outreach, accountability and administration of ordinances.[1]
>
> We believe in the local body as the visible manifestation of the universal body....Entrance to the local body is required and based on an act of volition.[2]

This definition identifies local Messianic congregations with other local bodies of Messiah of all backgrounds, the *ekklesia*, emphasizing the work of God in forming Messianic congregations. It also identifies the man-made structure for accomplishing congregational goals. Messianic congregations are part of the *ekklesia* as are all other local congregations that follow the Messiah, Jewish or non-Jewish. Along with the rest of the body of believers, Messianic congregations embrace the concept of union between God and one another in the *ekklesia*. The FMC statement of faith further defines Messianic congregations as bodies whose members are part of the universal body.

> We believe that all believers in Messiah Yeshua are members of the universal body and bride of the Messiah. The body of Messiah began at *Shavuot* (Pentecost) with the baptism of the Holy Spirit after the ascension of Messiah Yeshua....The membership in the body is not based on any earthly organizational affiliation but is based on faith in Messiah Yeshua. This body is distinct from Israel and composed of both Jews and Gentiles made one by the Messiah's death. These members are under the solemn duty to keep the unity of the Spirit and the bond of love with a pure heart.[3]

Organizationally, Messianic congregations follow no uniform polity. Some congregations have a plurality of elders without one particular leader, while others have a Spiritual Leader over elders and *shammashim* (deacons). Others have a congregational form of government. While uniform polity is not stressed among the different congregations, mutual accountability and concern is emphasized. As the movement develops, a more uniform polity may emerge.

While the FMC definition of Messianic congregations correctly identifies them as part of the *ekklesia*, it is not complete in that, while it explains how these congregations are like other local bodies of believers, it does not explain how they differ from other parts of the *ekklesia*. Any Baptist or Pentecostal congregation could meet this description. Even though Messianic congregations are one with the larger, non-Jewish part of the *ekklesia*, and have much in common with sister congregations that are non-Jewish, there are specific emphases that distinguish Messianic congregations from traditional churches. The FMC further stated that a *Messianic congregation has the specific emphases of:*

(a) expressing Jewish cultural forms at regular worship services
(b) observing the feasts and holidays of Israel in a Messiah-centered manner
(c) identifying with the Jewish people at large
(d) rekindling the understanding of the inherent Jewish roots of faith in Yeshua, the promised Messiah of Israel
(e) witnessing to the Jew first and also the non-Jew.[4,5]

Messianic congregations reflect Jewish cultural and religious forms in their worship to one degree or another, celebrating Jewish Holy days, and in many cases worshipping on Shabbat. Some have accused Messianic Jews of syncretism and deception because they choose to worship as believers in Yeshua in a Jewish manner. This is not syncretism.

Christianity and Judaism are not merely being combined like oil and water, which do not mix. Messianic Jews worship Jewishly because they believe it is perfectly consistent to believe in the Messiah of Israel and live as Jewish people. The Gospel itself came out of a Jewish cultural background. It is only because of the combination of rabbinic rejection of the Gospel and the anti-Jewish bias of the church fathers (see chapter IV), that Christianity and Judaism are perceived as mutually exclusive. Church teaching from the fourth century onward sought to separate Jewish believers from their own Jewish culture and roots. An ancient profession of faith required by the Church of Constantinople said,

> I renounce all customs, rites, legalisms, unleavened breads and sacrifice of lambs of the Hebrews, and all other feasts of the Hebrews, sacrifices, prayers, aspersions, purifications, sanctifications, and propitiations, and fasts, and new moons, and

Sabbaths, and superstitions, and hymns and chants and observances and synagogues, and the food and drink of the Hebrews; in one word, I renounce absolutely everything Jewish, every law, rite and custom....and if afterwards I shall wish to deny and return to Jewish superstition, or shall be found eating with Jews, or feasting with them, or secretly conversing and condemning the Christian religion instead of openly confuting them and condemning their vain faith, then let the trembling of Cain and the leprosy of Gehazi cleave to me, as well as the legal punishments to which I acknowledge myself liable. And may I be anathema in the world to come, and may my soul be set down with Satan and the devils.[6]

It is no wonder that Jewish people as well as many Christians have long considered Judaism and Christianity as completely divergent viewpoints. The ongoing, damaging effect of this viewpoint keeps people from understanding how Messianic Jews can believe in Yeshua of Nazareth and live and worship in a distinctively Jewish manner. Messianic congregations see no contradiction between Jewishness and Messianic faith. They repudiate the anti-Jewish bias of the Church fathers and the Jewish tradition that rejects the Messiah. Because the Gospel took place in a Jewish setting, and the Apostles all were Jews, they see no problem expressing their faith in Yeshua through their rich culture and Jewish heritage, pointing to those facets which point to the Messiah. They received these cultural forms as an inheritance from their forefathers. They are not outsiders pillaging Jewish tradition. On the contrary, they are Jews using their own Jewish traditions to express biblical truths pertaining to the One they believe is the Messiah. If it is legitimate for Reconstructionist and Reform Jews to reinterpret traditions to express their understandings, it is equally legitimate for Messianic Jews to do so, too. They do not claim to be Orthodox, Conservative, or Reform. They are up front about their beliefs, letting people know they are Messianic, and that they believe Yeshua is the

Messiah. This is not deception, but religious expression within Jewish cultural heritage.

Other accusations leveled against Messianic Jewish congregations are that they both seek to be under the Law and are setting up a dividing wall between Jewish and Gentile believers. Messianic congregations do not understand expression of Jewish cultural forms in worship to be a contradiction of grace or a wall of separation from Gentiles. Rather, they understand Jewish expression in worship to be redeeming those cultural and religious forms that express truth about God and his Messiah. The purposes of worshiping in a Jewish paradigm are biblical truth, cultural expression, and understanding the Jewish roots of the gospel.

Utilization of these forms is not for the purpose of erecting a facade to impress the Jewish community, nor for seeking to pervert Jewish religious symbols. Messianic usage of Jewish symbols is a legitimate expression of Jewish people expressing their faith in their promised Messiah. These worship forms may indeed prove to be a positive testimony to Jewish people that one does not cease to be Jewish when believing in Yeshua as Messiah, and that Yeshua is indeed for Jewish people as well as Gentiles. In this way, a clearer understanding of the truth of the Gospel for both Jews and Gentiles is promoted, indeed a positive testimony.

Yet testimony is not the sole objective for practice. The worship forms may have their roots in traditional Judaism, but the understandings of Messianic usage differ from traditional Judaism. Messianic Jews are not involved in the syncretistic practice of robbing Jewish forms of faith of their meaning and imposing a foreign meaning upon them. Rather, Jewish forms teach biblical truth about the Jewish Messiah, Yeshua. Using Jewish symbols does not mean accepting traditional rabbinic explanations, nor does it mean coming under their authority.

> A Messianic congregation is not under Rabbinic authority but is part of the universal body of Messiah, having been founded upon the apostles and prophets, the Messiah Himself being the Chief Cornerstone (Ephesians 2:20).[7]

Messianic Judaism is not seeking to become a *fourth branch* of Judaism. All three branches come from a branch of Pharisaism which is not accepted as authoritative by Messianic Jews. Messianic Judaism is a branch separate from the others, growing from the root and trunk of Biblical Judaism, a branch parallel to the main branch of the other three, separate from them. Messianic Judaism did not grow out of Pharisaic Judaism. It grew out of the Biblical Jewish faith of the prophets of Israel, as did Pharisaism. The point of commonality with the three branches of Pharisaic Judaism is the ancient Biblical faith and the common cultural and religious heritage. When dealing with the issue of tradition, like Yeshua the Messiah, where traditional Judaism does not contradict Biblical truth, it can be accepted as a valid expression. Indeed, tradition is not only a matter of religious practice; it is part of cultural heritage as well. When tradition contradicts scripture, scripture is to be followed. Messianic Jews are not under the authority of Rabbinic tradition, but under Yeshua's authority, yet with the freedom to reinterpret and adapt traditions to reflect the Messianic faith.

The precedent for reinterpreting traditional practice in light of Messianic understanding does not lie with the modern Messianic movement, but with the Messiah Himself. It was Yeshua at the Passover meal who pointed to the traditional elements and reinterpreted them in light of his sacrifice (Matt. 26:26–27). The Jewish believers in the Jerusalem Messianic community did not see faith in the Messiah as a nullification of Jewish life-style (Acts 21:20b–21). Paul himself did not understand faith in the Messiah to abolish Jewish culture and practice (Acts 21:23–26), but affirmed both as acceptable for Jewish believers. Culture, in relation to the gospel, may be understood as packaging. It is the gospel which is redemptive, not the culture. It is the contention of Richard Longenecker that Paul, in bringing the gospel to the Gentiles, repackaged the root Christology of the early Messianic Jews for his Gentile audience.

> But before the silencing of the Jerusalem church's effective ministry in the events of the sixties, the

Gentile ministry of the church had taken root and was flourishing. And although *the terminology was necessarily transposed to meet the concerns of another audience*, it was the christology of Paul, the Apostle to the Gentiles, which *continued the main convictions of that earlier mainstream faith.*[8] [emphasis author's]

Since it is the biblical faith and not culture which is essential to faith, Messianic Jews worshiping in a Jewish cultural context are able to pass on a rich Jewish heritage to their children, as well as a rich spiritual heritage in Yeshua. At the same time, through the very same cultural expression Messianic believers communicate the Messiah of Israel to the people of Israel.

There are groups comprised *primarily* of people who are not Jewish by birth, but love Jewish ritual and culture and believe in Yeshua as Messiah. These *Judeophiles* would not be considered Messianic by the Messianic Jewish movement.

Concerning the contextualization of the Gospel across cultures, Bruce Flemming made the following observation,

> Saphir Athyal, in this case discussing hermeneutics at Lausanne '74, likened the incarnation of Christ, the Word to the inscripturation of the Bible, the Word. Both, he pointed out, were Truth dressed up in the cultural clothing of the contemporary context....Instead of continuing the analogy and advocating modern incarnated Christians revealing God's new word for today, he talked of ways of communicating *that* truth....To be communicated....is a specific body of knowledge; a given amount of truth. Yet that truth is definitely influenced by the culture into which it is going. In this communication process the purpose is to make the information to be communicated *relevant* in every situation everywhere as long as the Gospel is not compromised.[9]

43

To understand Messianic congregations, it is important to understand history. Since the fourth century, Jewish people have been persecuted in the name of Jesus. Jewish history has been one of successive persecutions. Church history has been one of struggle, both in theological areas as well as in political areas. There is a history of violence that is intertwined with church history. Oftentimes that violence was meted out by those who called themselves "Christians." Messianic believers need to understand their place in that history, as well to articulate that place to both the Jewish and Christian communities. Messianic believers are caught in the middle. Physically, they are descendants of those who were persecuted, tortured, and killed in the name of Jesus. Yet, as believers, they are spiritual descendants of those *true* believers who dealt with the theological struggles.

There is a temptation for some Messianic believers to fully identify with Jewish history, denying the theological heritage of all believers. The problem with this view is that when there is a break with believers who have gone before one winds up struggling with the same issues they did. Rejecting their history puts one back at square one.

There is a temptation for some believers to break with Jewish history and culture, identifying solely as Christians. The result of this stance is assimilation away from Jewish culture and outlook.

Neither stance really works. The issue is not resolved by merely understanding what happened with those who went before, but in understanding the relationship of Messianic Jews to both Jewish history and Church history.

It should be understood at the outset that Jewish history and Church history are parallel histories. They happened at the same time and overlapped in various places, often tragically. There is an exhibit at the Nahum Goldmann Museum of the Jewish Diaspora in Tel Aviv. It depicts "Jewish Christians" living along side other Jewish people and even worshipping with them through the fourth century. This is when John Chrysostom, one of the church fathers, called the "Jewish Christians" to be separate from the Jewish people. We don't know how many Jewish believers actually followed Chrysostom's call, but anti-

Jewish attitudes of the Nicean fathers like Chrysostom further aggravated the split between Jewish believers in Yeshua and the Jewish people.

How very different things might have been for Jewish people had it not been for "Christian" anti-Semitism. What happened in Jewish history affects Messianic believers because it is their history. It forms, in part, the basis of the modern Jewish response to the gospel. What happened in Church history also affects Messianic believers, because this period contains a rich theological heritage, unfortunately overshadowed by the sins of "Christians" against the Jewish people.

Messianic believers are heirs to both Jewish history and Church history. They can not simply put themselves in one category or the other. What happened in the Jewish community affected them, as did what happened in the Church. Everything that transpired in both camps does not need to be accepted. Only that which applies to the specific situation.

From Jewish history, Messianic Jews must reject the traditional Jewish rejection of the Messiah. Yet, there is still much more which ties them into Jewish history and culture. It is their heritage.

On the other hand, Jewish believers, do not identify with, nor accept the anti-Semitism committed against the Jewish people in Jesus' name by the Church. However, much of the theological foundation shared with non-Jewish *true* believers in the Messiah should be accepted.

Some may say that they cannot have it both ways. This was the cry of Chrysostom and others. But, it is not Chrysostom they have joined, nor his organization, nor his church. They have accepted the Messiah who came to the house of Israel, as promised in the Holy Scriptures.

Messianic Judaism is not trying to roll back 2,000 years of history, but it does realize that God's truth cannot be changed by 2,000 years of human history. Messianic Judaism recognizes that God does not change. He is the same yesterday, today, and forever. If people swear falsely in his Name, it does not invalidate the reality of who He is, nor does it render unacceptable the validity of his word for us today. The same is true of the Messiah.

The fact that some people profaned his Name by committing the most grievous sins while calling themselves "Christians" does not negate Yeshua's Messianic claims. Nor does it render Jewish people who follow Yeshua as the Messiah promised to Israel non-Jews. When Yeshua returns and all Jewish people recognize Him as the Messiah, they will not cease to be Jews. Early recognition of Him does not make a Jew non-Jewish. It makes him Messianic Jewish. Yeshua is who He has always been: Israel's Messiah. His message today is as applicable to all Jewish people as it was in the first century C.E.

Endnotes

[1] Constitution of the Fellowship of Messianic Congregations, Article 3, Section 1.
[2] Ibid., Section 8, Paragraph 3.
[3] Ibid., Section 8, Paragraph 1.
[4] It is often said by detractors of the Messianic movement that they target the Jewish community with the Gospel, and this picking on the Jews is not fair. The fact is, the Biblical emphasis is to the Jew first. In reality, Messianic Jews seek to bring the message of Messiah to everyone, but with respect to its Jewish roots and applicability to Jewish people.
[5] Constitution of the FMC, Article 3, Section 2.
[6] Profession of Faith, from the Church of Constantinople: From Assemani, Cod. Lit., I, p. 105 as cited in James Parkes, *The Conflict of the Church and Synagogue* (New York: Atheneum, 1974), pp. 397-398.
[7] Constitution of the FMC, Article 3, Section 3.
[8] Richard N. Longenecker, *The Christology of Early Jewish Christianity* (London: SCM Press, 1970; reprint ed., Grand Rapids: Baker Book House, 1981), p.156.
[9] Bruce C.E. Flemming, *Contextualization of Theology* (Pasadena: William Carey Library, 1980), p.63.

CHAPTER FOUR

MESSIANIC SYNAGOGUE OR JEWISH CHURCH?

Messianic congregations are a recent phenomenon on the pages of ecclesiastical history, but they have a heritage that extends back to the earliest period of the New Covenant faith. Messianic congregations are part of the *ekklesia*, yet remain distinct from traditional church groups. It would be incorrect to claim a direct connection between modern day Messianic congregations and the earlier Messianic believers. Even so, it is clear that God is again calling out a remnant from His Jewish people to bear witness to Israel *from within Israel* to Yeshua the Messiah.

Modern day Jewish believers share a common heritage with those of the first four centuries. This end time Messianic movement is not the same as that which existed in the first century. Judaism and Jewish culture have changed. History has colored the wrapping of the gospel message in a manner that turns away many Jewish people before they can even grasp the content of the message. Just as the ancient Messianic movement was able to bear witness to the Jewish people of its day, so too the modern movement is now bearing witness to the Jewish people of today.

People unfamiliar with Messianic terminology refer to Messianic congregations as "Jewish Churches." They usually mean no disrespect. They are trying to fit the concept of Jewish faith in the Messiah into their own frame of reference. Their intent may be benign, but their choice of nomenclature may cause Jewish believers to squirm with discomfort.

Whenever someone uses the word *church*, a variety of images may come to mind. None of those images will be Jewish.

Some people take the idea of the *one new man* in Messiah, expressed by Paul in Ephesians 2:15, and assume the *one new man* is not a Jewish man. By default, then, the new man is a non-Jew. But Paul was talking about the new man in his new nature, reborn by the Spirit of God. As long as we are still in our old shells, the new man will still be man or woman, slave or free, Jew or Gentile.

Jewish believers are not trying to set themselves up as superior to non-Jewish brethren. They wish to express who and what they are in their own words. It is a matter of peoplehood and belonging.

The word *church* is a translation through Latin of the Greek word *ekklesia*, meaning *to call out*. Eric G. Jay defines *ekklesia* as...*a gathering of people who have been duly summoned, or called out.*[1] The term *ekklesia* is first used in the New Testament in Matthew 16:18, but is employed primarily by Paul in his epistles. He uses *ekklesia* to refer to the whole body of believers, everywhere (I Corinthians 1:2); a series of local assemblies (II Corinthians 1:1; I Thessalonians 2:14; Galatians 1:2); home groups and a local assembly in a particular place (Philemon 2; Romans 16:5; I Corinthians 16:19).

Ekklesia is a translation of the Hebrew word *Qahal*, meaning *to call*. In the Septuagint (a Greek translation of the Old Testament) the word used is *sunagoge* or *ekklesia*. *Sunagoge* refers to gathering or assembling together. Even though both words had secular uses outside the body of believers, either word, *sunagoge* or *ekklesia*, could have been utilized to refer to the gathering together of believers in the Messiah. Some argue that Paul's preference for the term *ekklesia* instead of *sunagoge* points to the fact that the church is to be something different from the synagogue, that believers should refrain from utilizing Jewish terminology and imagery in their worship. This would have strong ramifications for the Messianic movement which expresses its faith in a Jewish way. Jay observes four reasons why the term *ekklesia* was used to designate the community of believers in Yeshua:

> It is probable that more than one reason determined the Christian choice of the word *ekklesia*: (a) founders of early Christian groups, like Paul, must have known that in the Septuagint *ekklesia* was more frequently used than *sunagoge* to translate *qahal*, and that *qahal* and not *edhah* was the word used to designate official gatherings of the people on certain especially significant occasions; (b) *qahal* and *ekklesia* both have the consonantal sounds "K" and "L" and both have the root meaning of 'call'; (c) *ekklesia*...was not so distinctively Jewish as to be unsuitable for a society which quickly accepted Gentiles to membership on the profession of their faith in Christ as Lord; (d) the frequent use of *sunagoge* for the building in the town or village where Christians were increasingly unwelcome.[2]

These probable determining factors for choosing *ekklesia* over *sunagoge* are significant for the Messianic movement. Of the four reasons that the founders of early believing groups used *ekklesia* rather than *sunagoge*, the factors of consonantal sound and use in the Septuagint matter very little today.

The distinctively Jewish connotation of *sunagoge*, and the undertone of *sunagoge* as a building where Christians were not welcome, have a greater bearing on Messianic concerns. In the twentieth century, Messianic congregations do not call themselves churches, as do predominantly non-Jewish assemblies of believers. They call themselves either congregations or synagogues for the very reason that the term *church* is understood by Jewish people to be non-Jewish.

Many Jewish people associate *church* with a place where Jewish people are not welcome. Historically, anti-Semitism by the church fathers and persecution by Christian churches in the

49

name of Jesus during the Crusades, the Spanish Inquisition, expulsions, pogroms, and other acts of violence committed in the name of Jesus, have colored the term *church*. Father Edward Flannery has written,

> Did a Christian anti-Semitism exist in the patristic age? Despite the semantic contradiction, who can deny it? On the level of historical realities there appeared in this age an animus and violence against Jews that can hardly escape the definition of anti-Semitism. And although it in no way involved essential Christian dogmas but appeared as a lapse from Christian truth and love...from the Gospel message...it was sufficiently characterized by Christian trappings to distinguish it from anti-Semitism in other kinds of eras.[3]

Messianic congregations seek to share and live by the teachings of the Messiah without the excess baggage of things said and done in Jesus' name which were in violation of His teachings. Messianic congregations are part of the *ekklesia*. However, they refer to themselves as congregations or synagogues to reflect and communicate the Jewishness of the Messianic faith to a people who have mistakenly come to associate belief in Jesus the Messiah with anti-Semitism. Designation of local bodies as congregations or synagogues in the *ekklesia* communicates unity with all those who believe in the Messiah, Jewish or non-Jewish, as well as separating themselves from those who have expressed hatred and violence towards Jewish people.

Messianic congregations do not seek to define themselves according to what others claim to be. They express themselves in Jewish terms to express who they are. They do not represent themselves in Jewish terms to show they are not part of the Gentile churches. Jewish expression is very much a part of a Messianic Jew's identity and quite genuine in Messianic congregations. These are not Christians in Jewish clothing, but Jews worshiping their Messiah. If they were to represent themselves as anything other than Jewish, it would be misleading.

Messianic Jews are united in the Messiah to non-Jewish believers. The point of unity is not membership in the same organization or in having common rituals or customs. Messianic congregations resemble traditional synagogues more than traditional churches in their worship and liturgy. It is in those areas they have common bonds with other Jews. The commonality with Gentile believers is in the Messiah they all embrace.

Leadership in Messianic congregations is based on New Covenant scripture. Following a New Covenant model is not a departure from Jewishness. Since the New Covenant is Jewish, following its descriptions of leadership cannot be a deviation from what is Jewish. The model of church worship is believed by many scholars to have been adopted from the model of the synagogue.

The New Covenant speaks of bishops, elders, shepherds, and deacons; these lead congregations. Messianic congregations follow these biblical models of leadership in their polity. The titles used in Messianic congregations may differ because the connotations communicate a non-Jewish culture. Messianic Jews use different terminology to reflect Jewish culture. But people who fill leadership roles use the New Covenant definitions for their models. Scripture gives less regarding leadership job descriptions and more regarding character description (I Timothy 3 and Titus 1). Bishop and elder are used interchangeably at times.

> In Acts 20:17, Paul calls for the elders to meet him, but in speaking to them later he refers to these same officers as bishops. In…listing their qualifications, he states, *A bishop must be blameless.* [4]

Bishops or elders are to oversee the flock of God and to give account for the flock. They are to care for the flock of God (I Peter 2:25) and *rule* or govern the congregation (I Timothy 5:17, I Thessalonians 5:12, Hebrews 13:7,17,24). Elders watch over the souls of their people, that they might give account to the Lord. This leadership position is not to be a *lording over others* kind of leadership, but rather a serving leadership.

51

> *Yeshua said to them,* The kings of the Gentiles lord it over them...but you are not to be like that. Instead the greatest among you should be like the youngest, and the one who rules, like the one who serves (Luke 22:25–26).

The Jewish concept of a *shammash* fits well with the idea of Messianic leadership. A *shammash* is a servant, yet at the same time an overseer. The *shammash* in a synagogue sees to it that everything is in order. He is the congregation's sexton. The *shammash* on a Hanukkah menorah, is the candle above the others that bends over to light them; a servant to them, and at the same time the overseer.

Shammashim have a ministry of practical service. The Greek word *diakonos* (deacon) referred to household slaves who waited on tables. This office reflects the New Covenant concern for both the spiritual and material needs of people. I Timothy 3:8–13 records the qualifications of deacon, very similar to those for elder. The main differences in the qualifications of the two offices are in the areas of teaching and ministry to others. Elders exercise a ministry of teaching Scripture and dealing with people, while deacons have a ministry oriented towards practical service and assistance.

Shepherds, *poimenos,* are to *tend the flock of God among you* (I Peter 5:2–3). A shepherd doesn't spend all his time actively with the flock but watches it. They graze for themselves. A shepherd protects the sheep and disciplines them for the building up of the flock. Shepherds are types of the Messiah; Yeshua is the Great Shepherd (Hebrews 13). While Messianic leaders do not refer to themselves as *shepherds,* some follow the Christian tradition of calling themselves "pastor," meaning shepherd, while others follow the Jewish custom of calling their leaders "rabbi," meaning teacher.

A problem facing the Messianic leaders is that while the term *pastor* is an excellent job description, like the term church, it never gives the impression the title holder is Jewish. Those who use the title *rabbi* reason the leader of a Messianic congregation who has sufficient education should use a title that reflects both the position of congregational leader and Jewish identity. Some leaders use the title, Congregational or Spiritual Leader. The issue has yet to be resolved. Whatever term is adopted, the model for leadership is the New Covenant pattern.

Messianic congregations form the missing link between church and synagogue, bearing testimony that the Old and New Covenants are compatible; that "Christianity" and Judaism have a common ground.

Endnotes

[1] Eric G. Jay, *The Church—It's Changing Image Through Twenty Centuries* (Atlanta: John Knox Press, 1978), p 5.
[2] Ibid., p.7.
[3] Edward H. Flannery, *The Anguish of the Jews* (New York: Macmillian Publishing Co, 1965), p. 60.
[4] Robert L. Saucy, *The Church in God's Program* (Chicago: Moody Press, 1972), p.141.

CHAPTER FIVE

MESSIANIC JEWS AND THE LAW

The relationship between Messianic Jews and the law is an important issue in the Messianic Jewish movement. The law is not solely a theological issue to be debated. It is part of Jewish culture, heritage and worship. At the same time, Messianic believers recognize their relationship to the law is not the same as that of traditional Jews.

The center of a believer's life is not the law, but the Messiah. It is this shift in emphasis caused by the coming of the Messiah that raises the issue of what place the law occupies now that the Messiah has come.

It is important to understand Paul's teachings on the law. He addressed this issue directly in his writings. Unfortunately, many people have misunderstood what Paul said and assumed he was against the law. This misunderstanding has led to the idea that believers are to have nothing to do with the law. This became a sensitive issue for Jewish believers seeking to live a Jewish life-style while believing in Yeshua. A proper understanding of Paul's view of the place of the law is essential for understanding the place of the law for Jewish believers.

Before there can be meaningful discussion regarding Paul's teachings pertaining to the law, it is important to understand what was meant by the term 'law' in the first century. The word *torah* (law), comes from the root *yara*. John Hartley wrote,

The basic idea of the root *yara* is 'to throw' or 'to

cast' with the strong sense of control by the subject....The word *torah* means basically 'teaching' whether it is a wise man instructing his son or God instructing Israel....God, motivated by love, reveals to man basic insight into how to live with each other and how to approach God. Through the law, God shows His interest in all aspects of man's life which is to be lived under His direction and care. Law of God stands parallel to word of the Lord to signify that law is the revelation of God's will.[1]

Torah is translated *nomos* some 430 times in the Septuagint.[2] Hans-Helmut Esser observed,

It is important to note that *torah* frequently does not mean *law* in the modern sense of the term.... Originally *torah* meant an instruction from God, a command for a given situation.[3]

The word law *(torah, nomos)* may refer to the writings of Moses, the prophets, priests, judges, teachers of wisdom, regulations pertaining to sacrifice and worship, the book of Deuteronomy, and the Pentateuch as a whole.

Law is not a uniform concept. It contains history, poetry, prophecy, ordinances, commands, wisdom, apocalypse, and promises. Law, as current readers of the scriptures understand the term, is but one part of the Old Covenant writings, yet it stands for the whole.

Not only does the concept of law have a variety of possible meanings, but the Jewish people have changed their view toward it over time. Prior to the Babylonian exile, the law was,

...the rule of life for those who have been redeemed (see first commandment, which is the basis for the other nine)....The commandments were not a law, but an event, with which JHVH specifically confronted every generation in its own here and now....The law thus has a prophetic character.[4]

The original intention of the law was not to provide a means to salvation, but a rule of life for those already redeemed. The law is a challenge and instruction to teach *how* redeemed people should walk in the ways of God. This agrees with the basic definition of *torah*—to teach. The ancient Israelis were called a redeemed people because they were redeemed by the Lord from Egypt.

The law is not an instrument of salvation and was never intended to be so. Under the Old Covenant, people came to God on the basis of His *hain, hesed, and rachamim* (grace, mercy, and compassion). When David and Bathsheba committed adultery, the scripture does not say that he went out and offered up burnt offerings and sin offerings, but that he sought the Lord and threw himself on God's mercy in deep repentance which is explicitly shown in Psalm 51. David may have offered sacrifices at a later time as a response to God's forgiveness, but he was already forgiven. Isaiah 1:11,18 teaches salvation does not come from sacrifices, but from repentance, while trusting in the grace and mercy of God.

> *The multitude of your sacrifices—what are they to me? says the Lord....I have no pleasure in the blood of bulls and lambs and goats....Come now, let us reason together, says the Lord. Though your sins are like scarlet, they shall be as white as snow....*

Sacrifice alone was not powerful enough to bring atonement. It had to be accompanied by a genuinely repentant heart before God.

After the exile from Babylon, this original understanding of the law's purpose shifted in application. Esser says,

> This original view of the law changed in the post-exilic period, when the community was considered to be actually constituted by the law (Nehemiah 8). The law came to be viewed as a set of rigid rules, instead of serving the community as an ordinance of salvation.[5]

The Babylonian captivity commenced in 586 B.C.E., and according to the prophets occurred because the people turned away from the Lord and His *torah*. The returning exiles, fully aware of the reasons for the exile, living in the ruins of what was once a prosperous land, put a new emphasis on the law.

In the Judaism of the two centuries before the Messiah, through the first century C.E., the law came to be viewed in an absolute sense, independent of the covenant. It was understood to be eternal, existing from the foundation of the world. Fulfillment of the law determined membership in the people of God.[6] This, however, was not the opinion of all Jewish people. As far back as the intertestamental period, Judaism was not monolithic in its expressions.

Marcel Simon has said regarding first century Judaism,

> Judaism at the time of Christ had no universally recognized magisterium capable of formulating the norms of the faith. The duties of the priesthood lay in the area of ritual. The Sanhedrin was a court of justice whose function was to interpret and apply the law of Moses, rather than a council occupied with formulating doctrinal statements. Moreover, the Sanhedrin was far from representing a homogeneous point of view. The rabbis, who during this period increasingly assumed the role of spiritual leaders of the chosen people, also devoted themselves to the interpretation of the torah's stipulations. Their interpretations were made in the light of a tradition transmitted from generation to generation, although among the various schools there were considerable variations and even contradictions.[7]

In the first century there were many groups, but no one group was the undisputed representative of Judaism. Marcel Simon observed,

The Jewish sects were not radically aberrant groups vis-a-vis the official synagogue. Nor were they separated from each other....They were, rather, various currents that, taken together, constituted Judaism. Moreover, each one could claim, with some semblance of justification, to represent the most authentic form of Judaism.[8]

Present day Rabbinic Judaism has its roots in first century Pharisaism. While it was not the only expression of Judaism in the first century, it was highly influential and, apart from Messianic Judaism's rebirth in modern times, it is the only surviving representative of first century Judaism. Judaism of the first century was far more pluralistic than what has survived into modern times. The value of the rabbinic tradition in understanding what was understood as *Jewish* viewpoints in the first century is limited by the fact that the views of the other sects have not been preserved. From studying the rabbinic tradition, we get only a partial understanding of what was believed at that time. According to the rabbinic tradition,

> The word *torah* is variously used for the Pentateuch, the entire scriptures, the Oral Tradition, as well as for the whole body of religious truth, study and practice....To the Rabbis, the real *torah* was not merely the written text of the Five Books of Moses. It also included the meaning enshrined in that text, as expounded and unfolded by the interpretation of successive generations of sages who made its implicit Divine teachings explicit. This Oral Teaching was handed down from the earliest days by word of mouth until it was codified in the Mishnah circa. 200 C.E.[9]

The importance of this historical observation is the understanding that there were many differing views of Judaism, and the law in the first century, and belief in Yeshua as Messiah was not a departure from Jewishness or *torah*.

Paul wrote concerning the law in his epistles. In seeking to understand what he was saying, it is important to understand what he meant when he referred to the law. The question that needs to be answered in reference to the Pauline corpus is whether Paul was teaching that the law had no application for believers after the coming of the Messiah, or was he teaching that certain understandings of the law do not have application for believers in the Messiah. Leon Morris said,

> It is easy to misunderstand the place of the law, and it is Paul's contention that by and large his nation has done just that.[10]

By studying Paul's teachings it should become clear what he meant by 'the law,' and how believers must relate to the *torah* of God. Paul addresses the issue of the law mainly in his epistles to the Romans, Galatians, First Corinthians, and Ephesians, as well as historical references in the book of Acts. Paul's teachings about the law were in connection with other issues impacted by how the law was viewed.

In Romans 2, Paul discusses the law in relationship to the issue of justification. In verses 12–16, he says,

> *All who sin apart from the law will also perish apart from the law, and all who sin under the law will be judged by the law.*

The context of this passage is the judgment of God. Paul wants it understood that knowing the law is not a restraint against sin. There is a difference between knowing the right thing and doing it. The person who sins under the law is no better off than the person who sins without it. C.E.B. Cranfield has said,

> The main point made in this paragraph is that knowledge of the law does not in itself constitute any defense against the judgment of God....While those who have sinned in ignorance of the law will perish even though they did not have the law,

those who have sinned knowing the law...will be judged by God according to the standard provided by the law.[11]

Paul is not criticizing the law, but the attitudes of some individuals toward it. He is not saying the law is a bad thing, but that it is insufficient to keep a person from judgment. A central feature of Rabbinic Judaism is the study of *torah*. Study is important for its own sake in traditional Judaism, making knowledge of the law of prime importance. Rabbi Tarfon said,

> ...if thou hast studied much *torah*, much reward will be given thee, for faithful is thy employer in paying thee the reward of thy labor: and know that the grant of reward unto the righteous will be in the thereafter.[12]

In Romans 2:17–29, Paul expands on this topic by addressing a self-righteous attitude of those who rely on the law. Verses 17–24 detail this wrong attitude. The problem is not the law, but the wrong human attitudes people hold toward it.

In verses 25–29 Paul discusses the issue of circumcision in relation to the law. Circumcision for Paul has no value if a person is not living faithfully by the law. Again, as in verses 12–16, Paul's contention is that circumcision, like knowing the law, is of no benefit if it is not coupled with the accompanying actions growing out of an inward faith. A parallel passage is Galatians 5:3–6. The point is made

> *if you let yourselves be circumcised, Messiah will be of no value to you at all....every man who lets himself be circumcised...is obligated to obey the whole law. You who are trying to be justified by law have been alienated from Messiah; you have fallen away from grace....for in Messiah Yeshua neither circumcision nor uncircumcision has any value. The only thing that counts is faith expressing itself through love.*

Paul's difficulty here was not with circumcision in and of itself. If that were the case he would not have had Timothy circumcised. Paul's concern was with those who were trying to be justified by the law (which circumcision actually predates, going back to Abraham). Circumcision does not carry the burden of adherence to the law. However, the pretense that seeks justification by circumcision also requires adherence to the other commandments. Those seeking justification before God through their actions ceased to rely on God's grace through the finished work of the Messiah. Ernest Burton rightly wrote,

> The acceptance of circumcision is in principle the acceptance of the whole legalistic scheme. The reasons that can be urged in favor of circumcision apply equally to every statute of the law.[13]

Paul may have been responding to the attitude held by some within Judaism that circumcision, the sign of the Abrahamic covenant, would indeed insure a Jewish person's redemption in eternity. One passage of the Talmud says,

> Abraham's activity did not cease with his death. As he interceded in this world for the sinners, so will he intercede for them in the world to come. On the day of judgment, he will sit at the gate of hell, and he will not suffer those who kept the law of circumcision to enter therein.[14]

While it would be inaccurate to suggest that Rabbinic Judaism teaches trust in circumcision for salvation, this belief may have been present in Paul's time. Paul may have reacted in Galatians against Jewish zealots, or more probably Gentile believers who had themselves circumcised and were making much of it.

Paul is not speaking against circumcision itself when he wrote,

> *For in Messiah Yeshua, neither circumcision nor uncircumcision has any value. The only thing that*

counts is faith expressing itself through love (Galatians 5:6).

His point is not that circumcision is meaningless, but that in regard to one's standing before God it gives no special place. Circumcision is the sign of the Abrahamic, not the Mosaic covenant. The Abrahamic covenant is unconditional, having no requirements upon man, only upon God. It is an unconditional covenant of God's promise. Galatians 3:17–18 says,

> *The law, introduced 430 years later, does not set aside the covenant previously established by God and thus do away with the promise. For if inheritance depends on law, then it no longer depends on a promise; but God in His grace gave it to Abraham through a promise.*

Circumcision is a sign of God's grace to Abraham's descendants through His promises. Seeking justification through circumcision is seeking grace by works. Paul speaks against the attitude of those who seek to justify themselves by the law and its ordinances. In Romans 3:19–20, Paul says,

> *Now we know that whatever the law says, it says to those who are under the law, so that every mouth may be silenced and the whole world held accountable to God. Therefore no one will be declared righteous in His sight by observing the law; rather, through the law we become conscious of sin.*

The purpose of the law, according to Paul, is not that people be declared righteous by it, but rather to give people a consciousness of their own sinfulness. It serves as an indicator of where we are in relation to where we should be in regard to the will of God. This makes the law a blessing rather than a burden. This was expressed in Romans 5:20,

> *The law was added so that the trespass might*

> *increase. But where sin increased, grace increased all the more.*

The law does not increase our sinful deeds, but it does bring a consciousness of sinfulness which, in turn, brings a realization of God's grace, making us aware of how much we have been forgiven. This is not the law's sole purpose, but one of its purposes. It is clear that, from Paul's perspective, the law is insufficient to bring justification before God.

Coupled with justification is the concept of righteousness. Romans 3:21–31 explains the relationship between righteousness and the law.

> *But now a righteousness from God,* apart from the law, *to which the law and the prophets testify. This righteousness from God comes through faith in Messiah Yeshua to all who believe.* [emphasis author's]

Righteousness is testified to by the law, but is only obtained through faith. Justification and righteousness come through Yeshua, the atoning sacrifice for our sins. The law does not have a function in the attainment of justification and righteousness. Paul said in Romans 3:28, *For we maintain that a man is justified by faith apart from observing the law.* In verse 31, Paul asks, *Do we, then, nullify the law by this faith? Not at all! Rather we uphold the law.* Thomas McComiskey wrote,

> The phrase *apart from the law* seems to teach that the law has been nullified as a principle of obedience because the righteousness of God is now obtainable through faith. This view...is rendered difficult by the statement of verse 31....The solution...can be [grasped] when the law is understood to be honored by the righteousness of faith, to be fulfilled by that faith, and thus silenced in its condemning function because of the righteousness obtained through faith. The principle of law can

not give such righteousness; it is the standard of righteousness. When the standard is broken it condemns because it is law. But the law does not change human hearts. If hearts are to be conformed to the law, the change will be accomplished not by law, but by the revolutionary act of faith in [Messiah] which imparts new motivation and radical obedience.[15]

Paul is saying that what he has taught about faith is not inconsistent with law. Law does not nullify or diminish grace or faith. The teaching of the Old Covenant is consistent with the New. God's law is consistent with God's Grace. Paul goes so far as to say that this faith establishes the law. Everett Harrison expressed it this way:

The gospel establishes the law in that the latter is vindicated. The law has fulfilled a vital role by bringing an awareness of sin....Since the death of Messiah was in terms of God's righteousness, this means that the demands of the law have not been set aside in God's plan of salvation.[16]

For Harrison, the law is established by the New Covenant faith. Law and faith complement one another. The law is not without purpose, but that purpose is not justification and the obtaining of righteousness. In Romans 10:3–4, Paul said,

Since they did not know the righteousness that comes from God and sought to establish their own, they did not submit to God's righteousness. Messiah is the end [telos] of the law so that there may be righteousness for everyone who believes.

There is a difference of opinion pertaining to the interpretation of *telos* (end) in verse 4. One understanding is that the Messiah is the termination of the law, while the other is that

Messiah is the goal of the law. Daniel P. Fuller has observed,

> Understanding the *telos* in Romans 10:4 as *goal* or *completion* makes it easier for this verse to argue for the one preceding than if *telos* were construed as meaning *termination* or *cessation*....[Messiah] is the completion of the law in that, as Himself a revelation from God, he embodied in all his teaching and work a pure expression of the righteous standard of God found in the law.[17]

This interpretation makes sense in light of Romans 3:31. It would be a terrible inconsistency for our faith to establish the law on one hand and terminate it on the other. The explanation of Yeshua as the *goal* of the law is supported by Galatians 3:24, *So the law was put in charge to lead us to Messiah that we might be justified by faith*. It is also supported by the words of Yeshua in John 5:39,

> *You diligently study the scriptures because you think that by them you possess eternal life. These are the scriptures that speak of me.*

Thomas McComiskey wrote,

> If *telos* is understood to mean *goal*, then Paul's view is compatible with Matthew 5, where [Yeshua] demonstrated his goal of fulfilling the law by explicating it, defining it, and enjoining it on his followers. If Paul believed the Old Testament law was absolutely terminated, several statements of his are difficult to comprehend, such as his injunction to keep the law in Ephesians 6:2 and his assertion in Romans 7:25 that he was a slave to God's law.[18]

A practical question arose after 70 C.E. about the present viability of the law. The sacrifices could no longer be made without the temple in Jerusalem destroyed in that year. This question might be raised for anyone who seeks justification by the law. The rabbinic explanation was—and still is— that since the Lord left the Jewish people without sacrifices, only repentance and good deeds which accompanied the sacrifices are left to offer to the Lord. Others say it is not necessary to have sacrifices. What is necessary is that we only study about the sacrifices. These explanations do not adequately deal with the commandments regarding sacrifice. Believers have Yeshua as their atoning sacrifice. In this sense, the law has been fulfilled. There has been a termination of the need for further sacrifice. But sacrifice and justification are not the only purposes of the law. Paul wrote in II Timothy 3:16,

> *All scripture is God breathed and is useful for teaching, rebuking, correcting, and training in righteousness, so that the man of God may be thoroughly equipped for every good work.*

All scripture includes the law. In Romans 7:14a, 16b, and 22, Paul said, respectively, *The law is spiritual, The law is good, and ...in my inner being, I delight in God's law.*

Paul has not condemned or taken away from the law of God. He affirms the good of the law and its importance. He sees it as useful for believers today. He condemns the human inclination to seek justification and earn righteousness through the law, and does not want believers to embrace the law as a means of obtaining righteousness. He would have believers trust fully in the grace and promises of God for their salvation and justification. He sees the law, along with the whole of scripture, as profitable for training in righteousness and for equipping the saints, because the law is the revealed will of God.

Paul, in his epistles, affirms the law yet condemns the wrong emphasis men place upon it. In this sense he is turning believers back to the original intent of the law, it being a rule for godly living for those who are already redeemed. He rejects the later shift towards making it a means of salvation.

This is in harmony with the New Testament theme that the Messianic faith is consistent with the Old Testament faith and is its rightful fulfillment. There is a sense in which the law has been fulfilled in the sacrificial system, and there is another sense in which believers are to *fill it up* in their actions. This is similar to the concept of Inaugurated Eschatology. The Kingdom of God is here and, at the same time, yet to come. The law is fulfilled and, at the same time, yet to be fulfilled in believers living a godly life of faith.

In the context of Messianic Judaism, it is important to first differentiate between God's law and man's traditions. The two are not necessarily in contradiction but neither are they necessarily in agreement. Oral tradition surrounding the *torah* has become intertwined in Jewish culture. Messianic Jews may integrate certain cultural aspects of tradition into their life-style and religious expression without accepting the entire theological system behind them. It is most important when a tradition is incorporated that it have a clear meaning regarding biblical truth, and that it not be practiced merely because it seems to be a Jewish thing to do. The law may be a good criterion for determining how a practice may be incorporated. An example of this can be seen in Jewish dietary restrictions.

In addition to a distinction between kosher and unkosher foods (fit and unfit) on the basis of scriptural command, there is a detailed tradition, *kashrut,* separating dairy and meat products. This elaborate separation is based upon Exodus 23:19b, *Do not boil a young goat in its mother's milk.* This commandment is most probably an ancient prohibition against following Canaanite fertility rituals whose intent had nothing to do with dietary concerns.

Messianic believers may choose to avoid meats forbidden in the *torah* as a life-style and cultural identification, and yet eat cheeseburgers forbidden by rabbinic traditional law but not by scripture. While believers are not obligated to keep the law for justification, believers have the freedom to do so as part of a godly life-style. Paul's teachings reject the rabbinic emphasis of justification through works of the law which was never the intent of scripture. Believers must not fall into that trap, but must affirm the original intent of the law, to be a guide for godly living.

Tradition may be utilized for cultural identification, sensitivity, and to heighten awareness of the importance of reaching Jewish people with the good news of the Messiah. Tradition can also be reinterpreted to reflect faith in Yeshua. This is perfectly legitimate. The Messiah Himself did so at the last supper by reinterpreting the meaning of the Passover symbols in light of His atoning death.

Shabbat can be observed in a way that lifts up Yeshua, the Lord of *Shabbat*. *Yom Kippur,* the Day of Atonement, becomes a day of thanksgiving for Messianic Jews because there is full atonement in the sacrifice of Messiah. Fasting may still be part of *Yom Kippur* observance, but not for the believers' sins. Rather, fasting and prayer may be practiced for the salvation of the Jewish people, according to Romans 10:1. In doing these things the Messiah, the goal of the law, is lifted up.

Likewise, circumcision is practiced by Messianic Jews, not because it imputes righteousness, but because they are the descendants of Abraham, Isaac and Jacob. This is the sign of God's promise for all generations. It is a reminder of God's faithfulness, and the calling and heritage of Messianic Jews. They have the freedom in Messiah to celebrate His faithfulness through the rich heritage God has given. Messianic Jews may indeed be practicing the same customs and celebrating the same holidays, but for some different reasons.

Endnotes

[1] John E. Hartley, "Yara," in *Theological Wordbook of the Old Testament*, Vol. I, eds. R. Laird Harris, Gleason L. Archer, and Bruce K. Waltke (Chicago, Moody Press, 1980), pp. 403–404.

[2] Colin Brown, ed. *The New International Dictionary of New Testament Theology* English language edition (Grand Rapids: Zondervan Publishing House, 1980), s.v. "Law-Nomos," by Hans-Helmut Esser, p. 440.

[3] Ibid.

[4] Ibid., p. 441, quoting G. von Rad, *Old Testament Theology*, vol. I (1962), p. 199.

[5] Ibid., p. 441.

[6] Ibid., p. 442.

[7] Marcel Simon, *Jewish Sects at the Time of Jesus*, trans. James H. Farley (Philadelphia: Fortress Press, 1967), p. 6.
[8] Ibid., p. 7.
[9] Joseph Hertz, in *Pirke Avoth*, ed. Nathaniel Kravitz (Chicago: Jewish Way Magazine of Chicago, 1951), p. 31.
[10] Leon Morris, New Testament Theology (Grand Rapids: Zondervan Books, 1986), p. 60.
[11] C.E.B. Cranfield, *A Critical and Exegetical Commentary on the Epistle to the Romans* vol. I, 3rd ed. The International Critical Commentary (Edinburgh: T. & T. Clark, 1980), pp. 153–154.
[12] Kravitz, Prike Avoth 2:21, p. 137.
[13] Ernest De Witt Burton, *The Epistle to the Galatians* The International Critical Commentary (Edinburgh: T. & T. Clark, 1977), p. 274.
[14] Eruvin 19a, cited in *The Legends of the Jews* by Louis Ginsberg, ed. vol. I (Philadelphia: Jewish Publishing Company, 5728 [1968]), p. 306.
[15] Thomas E. McComiskey, *The Covenants of Promise* (Grand Rapids: Baker Book House, 1985), pp. 106–107.
[16] Everett F. Harrison, "Romans," in *The Expositors Bible Commentary*, vol. 10, Frank E. Gaebelein, ed. (Grand Rapids: Zondervan, 1976), p. 46.
[17] Daniel P. Fuller, *Gospel and Law: Contrast or Continuum?* (Grand Rapids: Eerdmans Publishing Co., 1982), pp. 84–85.
[18] McComiskey, *The Covenants of Promise*, p. 121.

CHAPTER 6

JEWISH BELIEVERS AND JEWISH TRADITION

A related issue to observance of *torah* is observance of Jewish traditions. An argument is made by those who are against Messianic Jews practicing Jewish tradition that while the commands are biblical and while it might be acceptable to adopt them as part of a life-style, Jewish tradition is not necessarily biblical. People who argue against Jewish believers following traditional Jewish practices raise concerns that those who follow those traditions are putting themselves under the authority of those who framed the traditions, that is, the rabbis. There is a legitimate concern when a person haphazardly takes on a traditional practice for no other reason than *it makes them more Jewish*. The fact is, no traditional practice will make a person Jewish or non-Jewish.

For example, if a person wears a *kipah*,[1] does he need a better reason for wearing it other than because he wishes to identify as Jewish? If a person has no better reason for wearing one than as a Jewish identification, someone could easily say, "Why do you wear a *kipah*, but not *tzitzit?*"[2] If he wears *tzitzit*, they may ask why he doesn't observe other traditional practices as well. Finally, after the individual is wearing and doing these traditional things, they ask, *So why do you need Yeshua?* The focus becomes tradition, and not redemption and relationship with God.

Traditional practices without theological foundations supporting them puts one in a vulnerable position. Some people reacting to this weakness have said that Jewish believers should turn their backs on all Jewish tradition. In doing so, they also are turning their backs on those things identified as Jewish.

Tradition is not a bad thing. It's that which was passed down. Tradition means heritage. A Jewish believer does not need to turn his back on his Jewish heritage to embrace the Jewish Messiah. If all Jewish tradition is shunned, what is left? When a person discontinues all Jewish practice, with what does he replace it? A Jewish believer is not to be a man without a culture. Every church has its own culture. It has been so intertwined with the worship, that some don't realize they have mixed their own denominational and cultural traditions in their religious life. For a Jewish believer to join a church, he must replace his own culture with someone else's culture. There is an alternative.

Another issue Jewish believers deal with is the use of traditional prayers in their services. Some say these prayers were formulated by the rabbis who rejected Yeshua, and are therefore inappropriate for Messianic worship. The fact is, some of the prayers predate the first century and may have been prayed by Yeshua and His disciples. Another factor is whether the prayer is seeking to denigrate Yeshua or his believers, or whether it is lifting up God in a way that Jewish believers can affirm. The issue is not who wrote the prayer, but what the prayer is saying and whether or not its message can be affirmed.

Other people complain that formal, prescribed prayers are lifeless. They prefer the impromptu prayers so common in believing circles. Most people who pray impromptu prayers fall into habitual patterns as they pray, with the same opening, closing, and order of supplication. A person can pray in such a way and have his mind and heart somewhere else. The real issue of prayer is not who wrote it, or how impromptu its composition may have been, but what the words reflect in the heart before God. A prayer composed millennia ago may express the desire and attitude of one's heart. An impromptu prayer may do the same. Prayer is the exercise of drawing near to God.

Another issue in Messianic worship is the use of the *tallit,* or prayer shawl, one of the symbols of Jewish worship. It is a sign of prayer and piety and is as much a symbol of the Jewish people as the *menorah* or Star of David. The *tallit* served as the design for the flag of Israel. On the four corners of the *tallit* are four fringes called *tzitzit*. The *torah* commands these to be worn as a reminder to keep the commandments of the Lord. A question arose as to whether Messianic believers should wear a *tallit*. For this question to be adequately answered, the meaning of the *tallit* needs to be considered.

The *tallit* is a symbol of prayer. It makes a distinction between the profane and the holy. It symbolizes wrapping oneself in prayer. It was not a *tallit* that was commanded by God to be worn by the Jewish people, but the *tzitzit,* or fringes. Numbers 15:38 reads,

> *Speak to the Israelites and say to them: 'Throughout the generations to come you are to make fringes on the corners of your garments, with a blue cord on each fringe.'*

They are tied in a way which points to the number 613, the number of the commandments in the Torah. They are tied this way because it says in Numbers 15:39,

> *You will have these fringes to look at and so you will remember all the commands of the Lord, that you may obey them and not prostitute yourselves by going after the lusts of your own hearts and eyes.*

In the ancient near east, the hem was ornate in comparison with the rest of an outer robe. The more important an individual, the more elaborate the embroidery of his hem. Its significance was not in its artistry but in its symbolic extension of the owner's person and authority. When David cut off the hem of King Saul's garment in the cave, Saul regarded it as a sign from God that his authority had been transferred to David.[3]

In ancient Mesopotamia, the upper classes would sign their legal documents by making an impression of their hem in the clay document in place of a signature. The practice in the synagogue of pressing the edge of the *tallit* to the Torah scroll while reciting blessings may be a vestige of this ancient custom. This act may have originated as a dramatic reaffirmation of the participant's commitment to the Torah. He thereby pledges both in words (blessing) and in deed (impressing his "signature" on the scroll) to live by the Scripture's commands.[4]

For believers in the Messiah, there has been a hesitancy among some to practice this ancient custom. To those who do not understand this practice, it appeared to be a form of idolatry, worshipping the Torah scroll. When it is understood that this symbolic gesture points to a personal affirmation and profession of commitment to walk by the word of God, there is no suggestion of idolatry. The Torah procession itself suggests that the word which was far away has been brought near and that by touching the Torah scroll with the *tzitzit*, it symbolizes the desire to personally draw near to God through His word.

The significance of the *tzitzit* is in the fact that it was worn in societies by people of importance. It was the identification tag of nobility. The requirement of the *tekhelet*, or blue cord, gives further support to this notion. The specific blue dye that was used to manufacture the *tekhelet* was from a particular snail and was very expensive. It was worn by royalty. It was the color of the inner curtain of the Tabernacle and the garments of the high priest. Weaving the violet-blue thread into the *tzitzit* enhances its symbolism as a mark of nobility. Since all Jewish people were required to wear it, it is a sign that God's people are a people of nobility. They are princes of God.[5]

The practice of wearing the *tekhelet* was discontinued by the rabbinic community in the period following the first century because of the extremely high cost of producing the dye needed to make the *tekhelet*. After several centuries, it was no longer known which was the shade of blue of the *tekhelet* of scripture. For fear of using the wrong color for the *tekhelet,* use of the blue cord was discontinued and only white was used in the fringes.

Most Messianic Jews who wear fringes use the *tekhelet,* considering any blue to be bluer than white. It is a sign as it was to the forefathers. The *tekhelet* in Messianic *tallitot* sets them apart from most traditional Jewish *tallitot*, and has become a Messianic identification.

The purpose of the *tzitzit* is to remind God's people to obey His word. His people are not nobility like the world's nobility, but are to be a "kingdom of priests and a holy nation" (Exodus 19:6).

Tzitzit are an exception to the Torah's general injunction against mixed seed. Mixing different material was forbidden to all Israel. Mixed materials were only allowed in the High Priest's vestments. What was allowed only to the High Priest, was allowed to all Israel in the *tzitzit*. It was a sign that Israel was to be a kingdom of priests and a holy nation.[6]

A. Palliere, a French Catholic preparing for the priesthood, sensed the true significance of the *tzitzit* when he entered a synagogue on Yom Kippur. He describes his experience with these words:

> That which revealed itself to me at that moment was not at all the Jewish religion. It was the Jewish people. The spectacle of that large number of men assembled, their shoulders covered by the tallit, suddenly disclosed to my eyes a far off past....At first on seeing the prayer-shawls uniformly worn by all the participants in the service, I felt that in a way they were all officiating....It seemed to me that this silent assembly was in expectancy of something to happen....In the service...all are equal, all are priests, all may participate in the holy functions, even officiate in the name of the entire community, when they have the required training. The dignity which distinguished the Hakham, the doctor, the sage, is not a clerical degree but rather that of learning, and of piety quickened through knowledge....rites and symbols often constitute a more expressive language than the best of discourses.[7]

To believers in the Messiah, the *tallit* and *tzitzit* point to their priesthood in the Messiah, and their personal commitment to live by His word with prayer.

A more fundamental question might involve the value of ritual. According to Emile Durkheim, a French sociologist, ritual contributes to the life of a group in four ways:

1. It enhances the solidarity of the group.
2. It builds loyalty to the values of the group.
3. It communicates values of the group to new members.
4. It creates a euphoric sense of well-being for the members of the group.

Ritual is that which binds people to one another. It binds them to their past. It binds them to future generations that will enter into ritual traditions. People do not even need to like rituals to derive a positive effect from them. Rituals build loyalty and commitment to values regardless of the attitude of those who are involved in performing them.[8] Their value is in what they do by affirming who we are and in connecting us to our past, present and future.

In Romans 14, believers are admonished regarding religious observances. Whatever they may be, they must be carried out with a pure heart before God. They must not be vain or empty external motions. Messianic Jews must not practice traditions just because they seem to be the *Jewish thing to do*. Jewishness is not magnified just because people do something traditional, neither is it diminished because they do not do traditional things. Jewishness is the result of physical descent from the patriarchs—Abraham, Isaac, and Jacob—and not the product of someone's actions. Being Jewish is a state of being. Either a person is, or is not, a Jew, and traditional actions will not change their status.

The problem with Jewish tradition for Jewish believers is not the traditions, but their interpretations. It is not very important who framed tradition. In the two Millennia of wanderings, tradition ceased to have solely religious meaning and has become part of the culture. It became heritage.

Jewish believers have every right to practice Jewish tradition because it is their heritage. It is right for them, and right for their children. It is important for developing a strong Jewish identity in children. The issue is not a matter of how much tradition to practice. Some will be more traditional and others less, the same as in the larger Jewish community. The issue is *how* to use Jewish tradition.

To simply participate in traditional acts because it is the *Jewish thing to do,* is no more than passing on a shallow practice to children devoid of meaning. To go through the motions of tradition because one thinks it will impress Jewish people with how Jewish a person is since believing in Yeshua, is at best a performance. But if traditions express faith in Yeshua, to responsibly communicate beliefs wherever they can appropriately be interpreted into traditional practices, then traditions become a means of communicating faith to children; they become a testimony to Jewish people. Most of all, they become a vehicle with which to draw near to the Lord.

In utilizing this approach to tradition, one can answer the person who asks why some traditions are done and not others. Messianic Jews see the Messiah in Jewish traditions. They agree their practice may not include the original meaning, but the actions express what is believed. As was pointed out earlier, it was Yeshua Himself, at a Passover *Seder,* who pointed to the *matzah* and the third cup and said they represent Him. Lighting *Shabbat* candles is not only to the Sabbath, the queen, it is to Yeshua, Lord of Shabbat, the Light of the World. The blessings over the *challah*[9] are to Yeshua, the bread of life. The blessings over the *kiddush* cup are to Yeshua, the vine of whom we are the fruit.

Within the Messianic community, there is a question of whether men should cover their heads during worship, in continuity with Jewish practice, or worship with uncovered heads, in keeping with the Christian tradition. Some people claim that wearing a *yarmulke* or *kipah* has its roots in the turban of the Aaronic priesthood. This argument says that the priests had to cover their heads upon entering the sanctuary of the Lord because they were uniquely in His presence in the Temple. They make the case that the Jewish people are a nation of kings and priests, holy to the Lord, therefore, should have their heads covered in His presence. In all fairness to the Biblical texts, drawing such a link takes liberties with scripture. While it may be acceptable to apply this concept to a present situation, it should not be taken as a direct application to believers today.

Those who oppose wearing a *kipah* or any type of head covering cite I Corinthians 11:4, *Every man who prays or prophesies with his head covered dishonors his head.* From a Biblical perspective, it should be recognized that while it misapplies scripture to equate the priestly turban with the *kipah*, it is equally wrong to claim that I Corinthians 11:4 applies to the *kipah*. The covering spoken of in this passage refers to a veil—a head covering concealing the hair and upper portion of the body.[10] This veil was worn by devout Jewish *women* of the first century.

Paul was speaking of wearing a veil down over one's head, saying such conduct dishonors the head, for Messiah is our head. The *Jewish New Testament* renders I Corinthians 11:4, "Every man who prays or prophesies wearing something down over his head brings shame to his head." What Paul had in mind was something that veiled the face and head. Moses veiled his face when he descended the mountain so the Israelites would not see the glory of God fade from his face. In the same way, Paul was indicating that believers are not to veil their faces. Instead faces are to reflect the glory of Yeshua. Paul was speaking in this passage of veiling.

The *kipah* does not veil, and hence, does not come into the scope of this argument. In addition, in the ancient world, a cap, or *kipah*-like covering, and not a bare head symbolized freedom.[11] In Jewish tradition, covering the head is a symbol of respect for God. This symbol of respect for God can be used to symbolize drawing near to God. By doing this, a distinction is drawn between the profane and the holy, between the worship of the Holy One and the secular world in which one walks.

On another level, the *kipah* is related to the *hupah*, the wedding canopy under which marriage ceremonies are performed. The *hupah* is symbolic of the presence of God at the wedding ceremony. It serves as a reminder that a marriage vow is not simply a contract made between two partners, but three.

God Himself is a part of the marriage and is a partner in the vow. A broken marriage vow is broken against Him as well as the spouse.

As the *hupah* is a symbol of being in God's presence, so the *kipah* is a symbol of being in His presence. It is a conscious reminder of the authority of God. The attitude of the heart is what matters. It may or may not carry the same meaning for traditional Jews as it does for Messianic Jews, but Messianic Jews are affirming what it means to them and not another group. It is a symbol of respect for God. Whether one desires to worship God with a covered or uncovered head, the important thing is to draw near to Him in worship together.

Practicing Jewish traditions in biblical conformity, Messianic Jews send a message that belief in Israel's Messiah is indeed compatible with being Jewish. Messianic Jewish life-style communicates that Yeshua is Israel's Messiah and should not be dismissed as irrelevant for Jewish people.

Endnotes

[1] Head covering, *yarmulke,* or skullcap.
[2] Fringes commanded in the Torah.
[3] Jacob Milgrom, *The JPS Torah Commentary* (Philadelphia: Jewish Publication Society, 5750/1990), p. 410.
[4] Ibid., p. 411.
[5] Ibid., p. 411.
[6] Ibid., p. 413.
[7] A. Palliere, *The Unknown Sanctuary* (New York: Bloch, 1928), pp. 20–22.
[8] Tony Campolo, *Who Changed the Price Tags?* (Waco: Word Books, 1986), p. 142.
[9] Ceremonial bread for Shabbat and special holidays
[10] C.K. Barrett, *The First Epistle to the Corinthians* (New York: Harper and Row, 1968), p. 249.
[11] Ibid., p. 250.

CHAPTER SEVEN

THE JEWISH PEOPLE, THE CHURCH, AND MESSIANIC CONGREGATIONS

An area of serious concern for Messianic Jewish believers is the relationship between the Jewish people and the Church. It is of special concern because of the prominent positions of both Israel and the Church in scripture, and the promises of God relating to both groups. Most theological structures attempt to overshadow the place of the Jewish people in God's plan. They incorporate the identity of Israel as the people of God into the identity of the Church to the exclusion of the Jewish people. Only recently has the place of Israel been addressed as a distinct division within systematic theology—a book by Arnold Fruchtenbaum, *Israelology: The Missing Link In Systematic Theology*.[1] It is the historic theological misunderstanding of the place of Israel in God's plan that has contributed to the schism between Israel and the Church.

Messianic congregations, predominantly composed of people who are part of both Israel and the *ekklesia*, hold a special interest in this subject. The Fellowship of Messianic Congregations stated,

> We believe Israel is God's special people chosen by him to be a holy nation and Kingdom of priests. The election of Israel is irrevocable, despite her

national rejection of Yeshua the Messiah. God will purge Israel of unbelief during the Great Tribulation "the time of Jacob's trouble," ultimately resulting in her national acceptance of Yeshua as her true Messiah.[2]

While not all Messianic groups would adhere to this theology, all do hold to the special position of the Jewish people in God's promises, and believe in and look expectantly for the eventual redemption of His ancient people.

The initial issue necessary to understanding God's plan concerns the identity of Israel. One view teaches that Israel was rejected by God for rejecting the Messiah, and has been replaced with a so-called *New Israel*, the Church. The Church is believed to have received all the blessings and promises of God, originally promised to Israel. The Jewish people (disinherited *old* Israel) is believed to receive only the curses. This "replacement theology" ignores Paul's words in Romans 11:29 regarding the stumbled Israel, that *God's gifts and his call are irrevocable.* It boasts over the branches which were grafted out, contrary to Paul's warning.

A variation of this view understands the Church to be a *New Israel*, without fully disinheriting the Jewish people. This view teaches that there will be a future time of salvation for Jewish people, but only as part of the so called *New Israel*, composed of Jews and non-Jews, in the Body of Messiah.

An alternative to these views is a position shared by many Messianic Jews and dispensational believers that the *ekklesia* and Israel are distinct. They understand there to be two groups, the Gentiles and Israel. Of each group there exists a remnant of believers, a Jewish remnant and a Gentile remnant. The Jewish remnant is the Israel of God, the Gentile remnant is the Gentile people of God. Together they make up the people of God, the *ekklesia*.

> We believe Israel is distinct from the body of Messiah. However, Jewish believers in Yeshua have a unique two fold identity. First, as the spiritual remnant of physical Israel and second, as part of the body of Messiah.[3]

The issue centers around to whom Paul is referring when he uses the term Israel. In Paul's writings, the word *Israel* is used seventeen times. Of the seventeen, ten unquestionably refer to the Jewish people. One of the questionable passages is Romans 9:6, *For not all who are descended from Israel are Israel.* It has been argued that this verse includes the Church. This interpretation is difficult to defend. Paul's argument following this statement moves from the broad to the narrow, not opening up to others, but excluding those not part of the remnant. He may argue otherwise in another passage, but here he makes the argument that not all Israel, but the remnant of Israel, are Abraham's children. This fits with the opening words of verse 6 that says, *It is not as though God's word has failed.* All Israel has not rejected the gospel, but as always there is a faithful remnant. *Not all Israel is Israel.* C.E.B. Cranfield says,

> Paul's meaning is rather that within the elect people itself there has been going on throughout its history a divine operation of distinguishing and separating, whereby *the church hidden in Israel* has been differentiated from the rest of the chosen nation. All Jews are members of God's elect people. This is an honor— and it is no small honor—of which no member of this race can be deprived....They are all necessarily witnesses to God's grace and truth. But not all of them are members of Israel within Israel...[4]

Another verse that illustrates the distinction between Israel's remnant as Jewish believers and the Gentile part of the *ekklesia* is Ephesians 3:6.

> *This mystery is that through the gospel the Gentiles are heirs together with Israel, members together of one body, and sharers together in the promise of Messiah Yeshua.*

The believing remnant of Israel is part of the one body with believing Gentiles, but they are still distinguished outwardly as are men and women. Gentile believers are heirs with Israel, but are not Israel.

A more problematic passage in determining the identity of Israel is Galatians 6:15–16. *Neither circumcision means anything; what matters is a new creation. Peace and mercy to all who follow this rule, even [and] to the Israel of God.* The understanding of this phrase centers around the function of *kai*, the Greek word for *and*. Either it connects two words with two different meanings or places them in a position where one explains the other. If the *kai* is understood as connecting two different concepts, the phrase *and to the Israel of God* would refer to Jewish believers. If *kai* is understood in an explanation-like usage, the passage would mean, *even to the Israel of God,* modifying *all who follow this rule,* i.e., the Gentile believers.

In favor of understanding *kai* as connecting two different entities is that this is the most common and natural use of *kai*. There is no grammatical reason to interpret the passage in other than a normal fashion. It is argued that in light of Paul's condemnation of *judaizing*, to interpret *Israel of God* as specifically Jewish believers rather than the whole body of believers, both Jewish and Gentile, would have given ground to the *judaizers* he wrote against. On the other hand, it can just as well be argued that since Paul had spent so much time in Galatians condemning *judaizers,* he was now affirming those Jewish believers who walked by grace, *the Israel of God*, along with *all those who follow this rule*, i.e., the Gentiles of God. Burton suggested the

> Israel of God appends a second afterthought. Though Romans 9:6, I Corinthians 10:18 show that Paul distinguished between Israel according to the flesh and the Israel according to the election or promise....There is in fact no instance of his using Israel except of the Jewish nation or a part thereof. These facts favor the interpretation of the expression as applying not to the Christian community as a whole, but the Jews; but in view of "of God" not to the whole Jewish nation, but to the

pious Israel, the remnant according to the election of grace....Upon those within Israel who even though as yet are unenlightened, are the true Israel of God. Against these reasons, the presence of the *kai* is of little weight...in view of the Apostle's strong anti-judaistic statements, he feels impelled by the insertion of *kai*, to emphasize this expression of his true attitude toward his people.[5]

Some have said that Paul refers to all believers as children of Abraham by faith. This is so, but all Abraham's children are not Israel. The Arabs are Abraham's children, but they are not Israel. Believers are not to seek the title and place of Israel, but are to seek to be children of Abraham by faith.

While it might be said that Messianic Jews have an axe to grind regarding the Israel of God, the accusation can be equally made of those who see the Israel of God as the Church.

Paul's love for his Jewish people, and his desire for their salvation can be clearly affirmed (Romans 10:1–4a). This is seen in the fact that God has not rejected the Jewish people (Romans 11:1–2), and the time will come when God will again turn, and redeem His people (Romans 11:25–27). Israel is not saved because of relation to Abraham, but must come by the grace of God to the Messiah.

Understanding that Israel refers to the Jewish people, it becomes important to understand the relationship between Israel and the Church. Paul says in Romans 11:28–29,

> *As far as the gospel is concerned, they are enemies on your account; but as far as election is concerned, they are loved on account of the patriarchs, for God's gifts and His call are irrevocable.*

The Jewish people are enemies of the gospel on account of the Gentiles, that they might come to faith. They are the gospel's enemies, in that they do not receive it, but they are most certainly *not* the Christian's enemies. Unfortunately, throughout the centuries the Church has committed the most horrible atrocities against the Jewish people in the Name of Jesus. The most common reason for rejection of the gospel by Jewish people is not theological. It is the historical anti-Semitic acts done in the name of Jesus. According to David Rausch, theological and ecclesiastical anti-Semitism set the ground work for the holocaust.[5] A common Jewish perspective to Christian anti-Semitism is reflected in the fictional work by Andre Schwartz-Bart, *The Last of the Just*. Schwartz-Bart, a French Jew, is himself a holocaust survivor, and here grapples with Christian anti-semitism.

> "Oh Ernie," Golda said, "you know them. Tell me. Why, why do the Christians hate us the way they do? They seem so nice when I can look at them without my star."

Ernie put his arm around her shoulders solemnly.

> "Its very mysterious. They don't know exactly why themselves. I've been in their churches and I've read their gospel. Do you know who the Christ was? A simple Jew like your father. A kind of chasid."

Golda smiled gently. "You're kidding me."

> "No, no, believe me, and I'll bet they'd have gotten along fine, the two of them, because he was really a good Jew, you know, sort of like the Baal Shem Tov— a merciful man and gentle. The Christians say they love him, but I think they really hate him without knowing it. So they take the cross by the other end, and make a sword out of it, and strike us with it... they take the cross and they turn it around, they turn it around, my God."[7]

In theological response to the historic relations between the Church and the Jewish people, Markus Barth has written,

> There is no excuse for the medieval acts of force and ruse by which Jews were subjected to baptism. As soon as the church acknowledges her dependence upon the first chosen covenant-people, she will do penance for the injustice perpetrated against Jews during two millennia. An authentic testimony to Christ and a persuasive demonstration of repentance are given only when the Christian churches do much more than simply *regret* or *deplore* what they have committed and permitted to happen. They are required to do all that lies in their power to see that discrimination, persecution, and murder of Jews is stopped and will never happen again. No longer can the church expect that Jews will be converted to and incorporated in a body that is still full of suspicion and hostility toward Jews. Nothing but the conversion of the church herself, can be the form and expression of the church's responsibility for Jews today.[8]

Barth's expression of grief and shame for the sins against the Jews is gentle and penitent. However, by his response of abandonment of the mission to the Jews, he overlooks the importance of Romans 1:16, of the gospel being to the Jew first, as well as the absolute statements of Yeshua Himself who said, *I am the Way, the Truth, and the Life. No one comes to the Father except by me.* Yeshua was speaking to Jewish people when He said this. If Yeshua is, as He claimed, the only way to the father, and the only means of salvation, withholding the good news of that salvation will not atone for the sins of the Church, and will leave the Jewish people without the Hope of Salvation which God intended for Israel. Paul said in Romans 10, *How can they hear without someone preaching to them?* In Paul's mind, the mission to the Jews was important.

A different response to Christian anti-Semitism is expressed by Catholic theologian Hans Kung.

> The weight of guilt is too heavy by far to be

balanced by...self justifications. The Church preached love, while it sowed the seeds of murderous hatred; it proclaimed love, while it prepared the way for atrocities and death. And these acts were perpetrated against the compatriots and brothers of him who taught the church: *What you did to one of the least of these my brethren, you did to me....*The Church that stood between Israel and Jesus prevented Israel from recognizing its Messiah.

The dialogue between Christians and Jews, if it is to be serious and not mere superficial fraternization, must be based on the Bible....There is no point in trying to overlook the real centre of controversy here: Jesus of Nazareth, who appears in the New Testament as the Messiah promised in the Old Testament and rejected by the greater part of Israel. There is no question of two "ways of belief" here...what divides us is Jesus, who is for us the Messiah, his death and resurrection.[9]

Kung writes with a great deal of sensitivity to the sufferings of the Jewish people, but with a more realistic biblical approach to dialogue. He hits the nail on the head when he recognizes that it is the Church that has come between Israel and their Messiah.

John Cogley, the religious editor of the New York Times, reported that a Christian had written the following prayer of apology to be read in every Catholic church throughout the world. The prayer reads:

> We are conscious today that many centuries of blindness have cloaked our eyes so that we can no longer see the beauty of thy chosen people (the Jews) nor recognize in their faces the features of our privileged brethren. We realize that the mark of Cain stands upon our foreheads. Across the centuries our brother Abel (the Jews) has lain in

blood we drew, or shed the tears we caused by forgetting thy love. Forgive us for the curse we falsely attached to their names as Jews. Forgive us for crucifying thee a second time in their flesh. For we knew not what we did.

The Catholic church chose not to recite this prayer. Its author died shortly after writing it. Its author was Pope John XXIII.

One reason the Church had become anti-Semitic may be that when people discuss *the Jews*, it is as a theological concept rather than as a living people. There is the strange absence of compassion in theology about the Jews. People read Paul's words of anguish over Israel and his heart's desire that they come to know the Messiah. They observe it but never take it to heart. If people would feel Paul's anguish and speak with compassion about Israel, perhaps there would not be so much for which the Church needs to repent. Yet love still covers a multitude of sins. It is never too late to show love, and communicate the real gospel message; the love of the Messiah Yeshua. For this to happen, the Church must begin to develop a genuine concern for Jewish people, whether or not they are believers in Yeshua. This begins by seeing Jewish people as people, not as religious or political concepts. It also means praying for the peace of Jerusalem, and for the well being of Jewish people everywhere. Such actions cannot hurt and may help heal the schism between the Church and the Jewish people.

There are many Christians who reject the charge that Christians were anti-Semitic. Their claim is that the people who perpetrated these acts were not *real* Christians, but were Christians in name only. In their view, a *real* Christian could not hate anyone, let alone commit such atrocities.

It needs to be understood that Christians, followers of the Messiah, still sin. Sometimes, believers sin in a big way. We acknowledge that Christians are not perfect. As much as people don't like to admit it, if they are capable of sinning, even being involved in serious sin, they are capable of anti-Semitic hatred and even hatred that could lead to the events of history.

Martin Luther led the way for the Reformation, yet he wrote

a terrible treatise against the Jewish people. Being a believer did not make him perfect. It is important for believers to realize their history in regard to the Jewish people, and to corporately and personally repent of it. Jewish people need to see the Messiah, and the Gospel, and not the sinful acts of anti-Semitism that have been committed under the guise of Christianity, either officially or unofficially. The individual believer may have no culpability in regard to anti-Semitism. It needs to be recognized, though, that when Gentile Christianity is presented to Jewish people, it will carry the stigma of anti-Semitism because of Gentile Christian history.

The reply of Messianic Jews to the issue of historic Christian anti-Semitism and modern attempts at dialogue is that they have not been persecutors of the Jewish people; they are part of the people. They are the prime candidates to share the Messiah with Jewish people. While all believers can and should share their faith with their Jewish friends, Messianic Jews can do what the rest of the *ekklesia* cannot—share the good news of the Messiah, *in house.* As part of Israel, the part that is redeemed in the Messiah Yeshua, Messianic Jews might be used to fulfill the words of Paul, *and so all Israel will be saved.*

Endnotes

[1] Arnold G. Fruchtenbaum, *Israelology: The Missing Link in Systematic Theology* (Tustin, California: Ariel Ministries, 1989).
[2] Constitution of the Fellowship of Messianic Congregations, Section 9, Paragraph 1.
[3] Constitution of the Fellowship of Messianic Congregations, Section 9, Paragraph 2.
[4] C.E.B. Cranfield, *A Critical and Exegetical Commentary on The Epistle to the Romans,* Vol. 2 (Edinburgh: T. & T. Clark, 1979), p. 474.
[5] Burton, *Galatians,* pp. 357–358.
[6] David A. Rausch, *Legacy of Hatred. Why Christians Must Not Forget the Holocaust* (Chicago: Moody Press, 1984).
[7] Andre Schwartz-Bart, *The Last of the Just* (New York: Atheneum Publishers, 1960), pp. 323–324.

8. Markus Barth, *The People of God* (Sheffield: JSNT Press, 1983), pp. 62–63.
9. Hans Kung, *The Church* (New York: Sheed & Ward, 1967), pp. 137, 140.

CHAPTER EIGHT

MESSIANIC JEWS AND THE TRI-UNITY OF GOD

One of the most controversial issues between Jewish people and believers in the Messiah is the triune nature of God. Some have questioned why Messianic Jews, coming from a strong monotheistic heritage, would accept belief in a tri-unity. Some assume that since many Messianic Jews have accepted belief in the Messiah because of efforts of Gentile believers, they have consequently accepted evangelical Biblical theology since it came along with the gospel message received from the Gentiles. This is an error of understanding and an over-simplification.

Messianic Jews have come to their conclusions and theological positions after examining the historical and biblical materials and concluding that they are correct. If what Messianic Jews believe coincides with evangelical theology, it is not because it has been inherited from evangelicals, but because the teaching is true.

Belief in the triune nature of God is not merely held by a group within the Messianic community, but is believed by every Messianic organization of the community: the Union of Messianic Jewish Congregations, the Fellowship of Messianic Congregations and the Messianic Jewish Alliance of America. A related area of difficulty for Messianic Jews is not the concept of the tri-unity, but the terminology. Trinity sounds catholic, and hence, non-Jewish. Tri-unity is an attempt, but is not really much better. There may never be a suitable answer to the semantic issue because there will always be tension between finding a word that is Jewishly palatable and one that is theologically precise. Of the two, accuracy is the most important, but palatability is also a concern.

Part of the problem in accepting this term lies in the fact that Trinity is a theological word, based on a biblical concept that bears no biblical nomenclature. If this were a biblical term, or if there were a Jewish equivalent, it would be more acceptable. Whether or not a word appears in Scripture, it should be considered acceptable as long as it accurately reflects the biblical data. The reason a formal trinitarian concept does not exist in the Old Testament is not because it is borrowed from Hellenism as some suggest. It is because the revelation of God is progressive. A full enough revelation did not exist in Jewish scripture until the New Covenant. The book of Hebrews tells us that *in these last days, God has spoken to us in His Son.* Yeshua is the ultimate revelation of God, and through Him we find the fullest revelation of God which we are capable of understanding.

The teaching of the tri-unity was first articulated at the Nicean Council in 325 C.E. by the assembly of bishops, presided over by the Emperor Constantine. Constantine was an anti-Semite, as were a number of the bishops. The conclusions of Nicea were looked upon by some as having a distinctively anti-Jewish bias.

It was at Nicea that the Christian day of worship was formally changed to Sunday. Christians were discouraged from celebrating Jewish Holy Days, in effect, cutting off Christianity from its Jewish roots. It was at Nicea that Messianic Jews were challenged to turn away from their Jewish heritage and be Gentilized, or risk being branded as heretical and face the consequences of that label. Many did. According to the historian, Fr. Bagatti,

> The writers of the 4th century always appealed to the council of Nicea, but regarding Palestine, represented by 18 members, we must say that the

Council knew nothing at all of the Judaeo-Christian current. In fact, all the bishops of the council were of gentile stock and represented the coastal cities. We know, e.g., that at this time there lived in Tiberias a Judaeo-Christian bishop active in the conversion of Jews, but his name does not appear on the list of the council. In fact the town appears in the conciliar lists only in the 5th century, when the Judaeo-Christians had been supplanted by gentile Christians....Their absence left a free hand to the capitulars, who could establish norms on certain subjects without meeting any opposition.[1]

There were Jewish bishops at the time of the council, but they apparently weren't invited. It is much easier to have unanimity when people with a different opinion are not present.

In spite of the negative aspects surrounding Nicea, it must be recognized that some good came out of it and some truth was affirmed. Among the good that was accomplished was a clear affirmation of faith. Because of the heresies which needed to be answered, the *Ekklesia* was facing serious theological challenges forcing it to examine its beliefs and define them in clear terms. It was for this reason that the triune nature of God was delineated, not because of an anti-Jewish bias. It is not the anti-Semitic attitudes surrounding Nicea that we affirm, but the truth that was articulated there, in spite of the anti-Semitism.

Another problem with the concept of the tri-unity of God is the antithesis it appears to present against the strict monotheism of Judaism. Some of the Trinity's opponents blame the Nicean Council's anti-Judaic bent for deriving a formula that would be unacceptable to Jewish people from the start. This concern is anachronistic because the concept of God's oneness had always been understood in broader terms than modern Judaism holds today. It could be reasonably argued that the Jewish understanding of God's oneness was interpreted more narrowly than in the past *in response* to the Christian understanding of God's oneness.

The fact is, the doctrine of the Trinity is not belief in three gods, but one God, who eternally exists in three persons, Father, Son, and Holy Spirit. Trinity is not a biblical term, but a theological one, seeking to accurately express all the data of Scripture relating to the nature of God. Some would say that the doctrine is not that important as long as one believes Yeshua is the Messiah. Scripture teaches that *if you confess with your mouth, Yeshua is Lord and believe in your heart that God raised Him from the dead, you will be saved* (Romans 10:9). While this is true, it does not teach that if a person affirms the right labels he will be saved. Rather it asks for the full acknowledgment of who God is. If a person acknowledges a Messiah who is less than Scripture says he is, he is not affirming the Messiah of the Scriptures. Affirming a Yeshua who is not God is not the same thing as affirming a Yeshua who is God, the Creator of all things.

Some have no problem with the triune nature of God, but have a problem with the concept of *persons* in the Godhead. The reason for the term was not to express three independent separate beings, but to guard against *modalism,* the idea that God is One, but takes on different forms, which would indicate that God is ever changing. Scripture, on the other hand teaches that God never changes. He is the same yesterday, today, and forever.

The Nazarenes, the first century Jewish believers who were biblically orthodox, were not the only sect which claimed to follow Yeshua of Nazareth. There were other groups who claimed to be Jewish and follow Yeshua as Messiah, yet their view of who He was fell far short of New Covenant teaching. Present day Messianic Jews are the theological descendants of the Nazarenes and not of the heretical groups that existed in ancient times. Yet, just as they existed side by side with heretical groups, so too in the twentieth century there are those who call themselves Messianic, yet their theology is not consistent with the Messianic mainstream. These groups and their beliefs will be briefly described below, followed by a discussion of Messianic understanding regarding the triune nature of God.

Irenaeus, who lived between A.D. 120–202, wrote concerning Cerinthus, a false teacher of the second century. He said,

> Cerinthus, again, a man who was educated in the wisdom of the Egyptians taught that the world was not made by the primary God, but by a certain Power far separated from him...He represented Jesus as having not been born of a virgin, but as being the son of Joseph and Mary according to the ordinary course of human generation, while he nevertheless was more righteous, prudent, and wise than other men. Moreover, after his baptism, Christ descended upon him in the form of a dove from the Supreme Ruler, and that then he proclaimed the unknown Father, and performed miracles. But at last Christ departed from Jesus, and that then Jesus suffered and rose again, while Christ remained impassible, inasmuch as he was a spiritual being. [2]

Cerinthus' view of Yeshua may have been a *high view* in human terms, but it fell far short of the New Covenant teaching concerning the person of Yeshua, as well as the role of God as creator. It is difficult to explain why Cerenthus and his followers would have held such a low view of Yeshua, except that Irenaeus tells us that Cerinthus was educated in the wisdom of the Egyptians. The New Covenant teachings of the nature of Yeshua and the Father may not have fit into the educational grid of Egyptian teaching. The views of Cerinthus and his followers were considered too different from the mainstream believers in the New Covenant community of faith in the Messiah. Consequently they were outside the camp.

Closely related to Cerinthian teaching was the teaching of the Ebionites. Ebionites, in contradistinction to the Nazarenes, rejected the writings of Paul, claiming he was an apostate from the Law. Also, they believed Yeshua was not divine. Origen, who lived between A.D. 185–254, wrote concerning the Ebionites,

> Let it be admitted, moreover, that there are some who accept Jesus...and yet would regulate their lives, like the Jewish multitude, in accordance

> with the Jewish law—and these are the twofold sect of Ebionites, who either acknowledge with us that Jesus was born of a virgin, or deny this, and maintain that He was begotten like other human beings.[3]

Origen was not unlike most Church leaders of his day who understood the theological distinction between Orthodox and heretical Jewish believers, yet lumped them together because of their Jewishness, and similar life-styles. This is as wrong as lumping Mormons and Evangelical Christians together because they both claim to follow Jesus Christ, when the way each follows Jesus is radically different from the other.

Those who call themselves Messianic, yet reject New Covenant teaching, cannot be rightly called Messianic. Messianic Jews accept the Old and New Covenants as authoritative in all matters of faith and practice. The Yeshua these modern-day heretics follow is not the Yeshua taught of in New Covenant. The Yeshua of Messianic Judaism is fully man, yet fully God. He is the creator of all things, was incarnated and virgin born, and has always existed.

A group that was closely related to the Ebionites was the Elkesaites. According to the second century historian, Hippolytus, Elkesai taught that,

> Christ was born a man in the same way that is common to all and that Christ was not for the first time on earth when born of a virgin, but that both previously and that frequently again He had been born, and would be born. Christ would thus appear and exist among us from time to time...[4]

This group not only affirmed the Virgin birth, but saw it as a recurring event, yet denied the deity of Yeshua.

One final group, the followers of Sabellius, believed in One God in three temporary manifestations. This is also called modalism. According to Epiphanius,

...a certain Sabellius came to the fore. Their doctrine is, that Father, Son, and Holy Spirit are one and the same being, in the sense that three names are attached to one substance.[5]

All these groups claimed to be Jewish followers of Yeshua, but their understandings of who Yeshua is differed greatly. Some had problems with reconciling the Oneness of God with the divinity of Yeshua, while others had problems with issues of the Torah. These are issues that Jewish believers struggle with today. As God has raised up the Messianic movement once again in these end days, so too have the counterfeits arisen, as in the beginning. The reason for discussing the issue of the triune nature of God, is the same as it has always been. It is an important issue.

Affirming faith in Yeshua necessitates an understanding of who Yeshua really is. To call on the name of the Lord is not the chanting of a mantra, but rather acknowledgment of the true nature of God. Calling on a Yeshua who is not divine is calling into the wind. Calling on Yeshua, the divine Son of God, Lord of all, is salvation.

Modalism is another theological error made by believers. It is the simplest attempt to explain the triune nature of God while preserving the oneness of God. This error is particularly appealing to those who seek to affirm the Oneness of God which is foundational to the Judaism of the Torah as well as the teachings of the New Covenant. Concerning modalism, eminent theologian, Harold O.J. Brown has written

> Modalism upholds the deity of *Yeshua,* but does not see Him as a distinct Person in regard to the Father. It holds that God reveals himself under different aspects or modes in different ages—as the Father in Creation and in the giving of the Law, as the Son in the *Messiah Yeshua,* and as the Holy Spirit after *Messiah's* ascension. Modalism stresses the full deity of the *Messiah* and...avoids the suggestion that he is a second God alongside

the Father. Unfortunately, it abandons the diversity of Persons within the Godhead, and thus loses the important concept that *the Messiah* is our representative or advocate with the Father.

Logically, modalism makes the events of redemptive history a kind of charade. Not being a distinct person, the Son cannot really represent us to the Father. Modalism must necessarily....teach that *Messiah* was human in appearance only; the alternative, on the basis of modalistic presuppositions, is that God himself died on the Cross. Since such an idea is considered absurd...the normal consequence is the conclusion that while the Messiah was fully God, he only appeared to be man.[6]

The modalists emphasize the Gospel of John with its statements stressing the oneness of Yeshua with the Father, for example, *I and my Father are One*....The word *one* in the Greek text of John 10:30 is the neuter *hen*, which suggests that the meaning is "one deity, one divine essence," rather than one Person. If the Son is not a real person who can stand before the Father and address him, then the....concept of substitutionary sacrifice, which holds that Yeshua takes our place and pays our debt to the Father, becomes at best a symbol and not a reality. Where modalism prevails, the concept of substitutionary satisfaction, or vicarious atonement, will necessarily be absent, and so modalism is sometimes adopted by those who object to the doctrine of vicarious atonement. More commonly, however, it simply arises as an attempt to reduce the mystery of the trinity to a more understandable concept, even at the cost of the true humanity of Yeshua and the doctrine of substitutionary satisfaction.[7]

The problem Messianic Jews face is the problem all believers face: explaining the faith. No matter from what perspective one tries to explain, faith is a mystery. The solution is to affirm the truths of Scripture concerning God, leaving further explanation to mystery. In other words, affirm that God is One and eternally exists in three persons—Father, Son and Spirit, without seeking to explain *how* this can be.

This position does not mean that the concept is illogical, only that it transcends one's ability to comprehend the nature of God. It is presumptuous to assume that finite human beings can fully grasp the infinite God. It is wisdom to acknowledge limitations. Affirm the truth one *can* grasp rather than seeking to explain things that go beyond one's comprehension. It is a far weaker position to attempt an explanation of that which one is unable to explain than to give an interpretation that falls short of Biblical truth.

Some have pointed out that there is a need for a different explanation of the triune nature of God. Jewish people find the tri-unity be conflict with Judaism's monotheism. This is a fallacy. As Dr. Brown wrote,

> Orthodox trinitarian doctrine is summarized in the definition, *One essence* [or nature, substance] *in three Persons.* There is but one God, as the Jewish *Shema* affirms (Deut. 6:4), for there is only one divine essence. This essence subsists in three distinct subjects or Persons....The divine Persons are distinct, yet they cannot be separated from the godhead or from one another. It is apparent that human language is inadequate to do much more than to suggest the nature of the Trinity; it certainly cannot analyze it or explain it.[8]

When dealing with the doctrine of the tri-unity of God, the main problem is the nature of the doctrine, not its teachings. The Nicean church fathers expressed Biblical truths in a credal format, seeking to summarize Biblical data. The approach they took was based upon Greek philosophical formations. The Nicean bishops were accustomed to the deductions of philosophical reasoning. The bishops thought that in shedding the Jewishness of the Gospels, they were freeing the message from the constraints of Jewish heritage and thought. They failed to realize that in freeing the message in this way, they bound it in pagan Greek hellenistic philosophy. While the product they produced reflected biblical truths, the way it was couched was anything but Jewish, and was most unpalatable to Jewish people.

Attempts have been made in the past to express the doctrine of the tri-unity in Jewish terms, but they simply were no more than semantic variations that did not approach the hellenistic format of the doctrine. Others have become frustrated and repudiated the doctrine. As we have seen, when that happens, there is nothing to prevent the distorted views of earlier heresies.

Hellenism sought, through philosophical formulations, to deduce, principalize and credalize the truth. They arrived at the truth, and deduced it to a creed. This was not Jewish in form.

From the New Testament and early Messianic apocryphal writings, one can see non-credal methods of expressing the truth through *testimonia*. They have been dismissed as incomplete methods because they do not end in credal forms. Yet *testimonia* is biblical, and presents the truth in a manner which is non-credal, and, hence, non-hellenistic. *Testimonia* is the biblical testimony to the identity of Yeshua. Rather than saying Yeshua is God, *testimonia* would say, Scripture says,

> *In the beginning was the Word, and the Word was with God, and the Word was God....The Word became a human being and lived with us, and we saw his* Sh'khinah, *the* Sh'khinah *of the Father's only Son, full of grace and truth* (Yochanan—John 1:1,14).

The conclusion would be that Yeshua is God, but rather than citing the conclusion, the Scripture is cited. Scripture can be cited to teach the full humanity and full divinity of Yeshua, the divinity and person of the Holy Spirit, and their separateness and unity with the Father. The doctrine of the tri-unity is a doctrine that sums up the *testimonia*, but the *testimonia* is what is used to support the doctrine. Messianic Jews might do better to affirm the doctrine of the tri-unity, but to do no more than realize it is the conclusion of the *testimonia* of Scripture. When speaking to Jewish people, seeking to teach and express Messianic beliefs, Messianic Jews might do well to emphasize the *testimonia* themselves, and give recognition to the biblical conclusions expressed in the creeds. The purpose of the doctrine of the tri-unity was to teach and safeguard the truth of one God, eternally existing as Father, Son, and Holy Spirit. If this can be accomplished through the use of *testimonia* rather than credal forms, much dispute and controversy may be avoided.

Believers in the Messiah must address to Jewish people the Messiahship of Yeshua. The doctrine of the tri-unity is not an apologetic; it is an explanation. People may object to its language, but the fact is, it does not teach the existence of three deities. The tri-unity is not inconsistent with the *Shema* or any other concept of biblical Judaism. The idea of three persons in the godhead is well within the concept of Jewish thought. It is taught by the *Zohar* (a book of Jewish mysticism).[9]

Holding to belief in One God, eternally existing in three Persons, is not polytheism. It is not beyond the pale of Jewish thought, and most importantly, it is the teaching of Scripture. Accepting this biblical belief does not diminish Jewishness. Jewishness is heritage. What Messianic Jews believe is based on God's revelation in His Messiah. The traditional Jewish view of God without the Messiah is incomplete. The Messiah is the key to understanding the Scripture. He is the fullest revelation of God.

Endnotes

[1] Fr. Bellarmino Bagatti, *The Church from the Circumcision* (Jerusalem: Franciscan Printing Press, 1984), pp. 86-87.
[2] Irenaeus, *Against Heresies*, I 26, 1.
[3] Origen, *Against Celsus*, V,61.
[4] Hippolytus, *The Refutation of All Heresies*, IX.
[5] Epiphanius, *Against Heresies*, LXII, I.
[6] Harold O.J. Brown, *Heresies: The Image of Christ in the Mirror*

of Heresy and Orthodoxy from the Apostles to the Present (Grand Rapids: Baker Book House, 1984), p. 99.
7   Ibid., p. 100.
8   Ibid., p. 146.
9   Rabbi Tzvi Nassi, *The Great Mystery: How Can Three Be One?* (Cincinnati: Messianic Literature Outreach, 1990).

CHAPTER NINE

MESSIANIC JUDAISM: A PIONEER MOVEMENT

Membership in a Messianic congregation differs in several respects from membership in a traditional church or synagogue. Messianic congregations are smaller than most churches and synagogues. There is a sense of close community shared by their members. Messianic congregations tend to be *non-churchy* because they express Jewish cultural patterns in worship. The reason Messianic congregations worship in a Jewish worship style is because most members are Jewish and the cultural expression of the congregation reflects the membership. It is legitimate for people to worship the Lord in their own cultural context. Those members who are not Jewish share a desire to identify with the Jewish people and their calling. They find membership in a Messianic congregation an ideal opportunity to identify with the Jewish people as did Ruth, who said to Naomi, *Do not urge me to leave you or to turn back from you. Where you go I will go, and where you stay, I will stay. Your people will be my people, and your God my God.*

Although most people who attend Messianic congregations have sincere motives, some people who attend do not come because they have a desire to identify with the Jewish people or feel called to be part of a Messianic congregation. A small minority come because they are anti-church. Since Messianic congregations do not have crosses, hymnals or other church symbols, they think they have found a place they can express their non-church sentiment. Messianic congregations seek to positively express Jewishness in their worship, but do not seek to be anti-church or anti-Gentile. Such people do not have a calling to Messianic congregations. They come for the wrong reasons and are counter-productive to congregations moving forward.

In a sense, those who are part of a Messianic congregation have a pioneering spirit. Messianic Judaism is a growing movement. By comparison with the larger body of believers Messianic congregations are small. Often, they don't have the attendance that more traditional congregations do. Most Messianic congregations can't offer huge buildings, ornate surroundings, or dazzling programs. Yet to those who are called to Messianic Judaism, the external factors are not the only things that are considered.

Messianic congregations are part of how God is working with the Jewish people. The experience of being part of the Messianic movement is not too different from the situation of the Jewish people in the days of Nehemiah.

Nehemiah records events that took place 90 years after the return from Babylon. Jerusalem was destroyed in 586 B.C.E. The events of this book take place around 433, almost 160 years after Jerusalem was destroyed. In this time, Daniel lived and died. Esther was queen of Persia and died. Artaxerxes succeeded Ahausuerus (Xerxes) as king of Persia. Zerubbabel had led the first captives back to Israel, and the Temple of the Lord had been rebuilt. Nehemiah was part of the second or third generation of Jewish people to stay in the dispersion after the Lord brought back the captives from Babylon. At that time, most of the Jewish people lived in the exile. They made homes for themselves, had businesses, and occupied positions of authority with the heathens among whom they lived.

Not everyone came back to Zion. Most did not. Nehemiah was one who stayed behind—for a time. He had a position of authority as cupbearer to the King of Persia. The significance of Nehemiah's life was not his position, but his interest in those who returned to Israel. His brother Hanani came back from a visit to Judah. Nehemiah inquired about his people. He was concerned for them.

They were the returning remnant. They were the pioneers, the ones willing to leave the comforts of large pagan cities to live in the land God promised to the Jewish people. For them to live in Israel meant giving up comforts.

At one time Jerusalem was the jewel of the middle east, but it had been devastated. Living there meant they would have a hard life. In spite of this, they chose to live in the Land of Israel. They moved there because it was theirs. They were not foreigners or strangers in Israel. By living in the land God promised they were partaking of the promise God made to Abraham. Living in Israel they declared the faithfulness of God to the Jews in exile, and also to the world.

Jewish believers in Messianic congregations experience a similar feeling when they are part of a Messianic congregation instead of a traditional church. In churches, Jewish believers are the foreigners; the ones who are different. Sometimes they are put on pedestals and paraded around as spiritual trophies; Sometimes they are asked to deny their Jewishness and conform to the oneness of the church. In a Messianic congregation, Jewish believers are not treated as different or special because they are Jewish. In a Messianic congregation they are neither different or more special than anyone else. They are treated as they should be: part of the community of faith.

Nehemiah's interest in those who returned to Judah is much the same as modern American Jews concern about Israel. He was concerned for his people's welfare. Nehemiah was a Zionist.

Nehemiah's brother reported that, *Those who survived the exile and are back in the province are in great trouble and disgrace. The Wall of Jerusalem is broken down, and it's gates have been burned by fire.* Jerusalem and Judah as a whole were run down. Nehemiah was astonished to hear about the situation.

This should not have been a shock to Nehemiah. It had been over 150 years since the Babylonian devastation. He knew that Jerusalem had been long destroyed. On the other hand, Nehemiah also knew that Zerubbabel had rebuilt the temple, and Ezra had restored religious order. From the information he had, Nehemiah had reason to believe that Jerusalem was in fine condition. When he heard how bad conditions were, he wept, mourned, fasted and prayed before the God of heaven.

The people in the land were only a remnant of Israel's people. Their living was simple. Their rebuilt temple was only a shadow of what once was. The city walls were broken down. Compared to the beautiful cities of Babylon and Shushan, Jerusalem was a reproach.

In a similar way, Messianic Judaism has been a reproach until recent years. But things are changing as in the days of Nehemiah.

There is another parallel between Nehemiah's situation and the Messianic movement. Those who are part of the Messianic congregations are a remnant. They are not in the days when it can be said, as it was in Acts 2:46, *Every day they continued to meet together in the temple courts.* They don't have many thousands all meeting together in the Temple. Messianic congregations do not represent all Jewish people. They are only a remnant of Israel. They do not represent all Jewish believers. They are a remnant of the Jewish believers. Many Jewish believers are in churches. They do not feel called to be part of the Messianic movement. Some do not want to leave the comfort of established congregations and ornate buildings. Some have no interest in Messianic Judaism or in their Jewish identities. They may visit, but they give a report like Nehemiah's brother. They look around but do not want to join.

Nehemiah had a different attitude. When he heard of the conditions in Judah and Jerusalem, he grieved and prayed. He was burdened for his people and for the remnant in the Land. Nehemiah cared enough to do something about the situation. He was willing to leave his position and the comforts of Shushan to go to Jerusalem to rebuild it.

Nehemiah is a picture of the kind of person who is called to a Messianic congregation. He is not the kind of person who comes, visits and turns away. He is not a person who visits to gain a nostalgic look at his old Jewish heritage. He is the kind of person who seeks to rebuild the walls. This kind of person is not looking to oppose something else but seeking to positively build up and encourage others. He invests his time and effort to serve the Lord. Such a person is a great encouragement to others.

This was the effect Nehemiah had on those around him. When they heard of Nehemiah's burden and how the Lord had provided, the people began the work. They were behind him and cooperated in the rebuilding effort.

The Jewish people's reaction was not the only response to Nehemiah. He was opposed by Sanballat the Horonite, Tobiah the Ammonite, and Geshem the Arab. Nehemiah wasn't swayed by these detractors. He knew the Lord was with him, and that he had the authority of the king to perform what was before him. He was determined to do the work the Lord had given him.

This, too, is a parallel to the Messianic movement. God may indeed put it on people's hearts to build up the congregations, but there is always someone who seeks to tear them down. These people always claim to have righteous motives. They are willing to help with suggestions, but never to get actively involved in building up. Sanballat said that he was just trying to protect the king's interests. Those who are called to be part of Messianic congregations will manifest that calling in their desire to build up the congregation through service and outreach.

As Nehemiah records the task of rebuilding the walls, he lists the people who worked on each section of the wall. The list is diverse. This is not the Bible's version of name plates, where a person is recognized for donating something to a church or synagogue. A plaque is mounted stating who made the donation or in who's honor the donation is made. The names recorded by Nehemiah teach something important.

Scripture teaches that the high priest and his fellow priests rebuilt the sheep gate. The men of Jericho built another section. The fish gate was rebuilt by the sons of Hassenaah. Individuals worked on other sections alone. The men of Tekoa built another section, but it says their nobles wouldn't work. The passage records that goldsmiths, perfume-makers and rulers of districts all worked on the wall. One man worked with his daughters. The ruler of Beth Haccerem, leaders, temple servants, guards, merchants and Levites are all listed. Everyone worked. Some built large sections, others worked on sections near their own homes. The attitude of the people is striking. Each one, except for the nobles of Tekoa, worked on the wall. Some may have had experience in building. Others clearly did not. Yet they all worked on rebuilding the walls of Jerusalem.

The wall was important for several reasons. Until modern times, walls were the main defense against attack in times of war. With the wall destroyed, anyone could enter a city and ravage and ransack it. That is why conquering armies always destroyed the walls of a city.

Secondly, the wall was a symbol. It served as a reminder that Jerusalem was destroyed, and that Israel was still a humbled people. Every time they looked at the rubble, it was a reminder of weakness and destruction.

Rebuilding the wall meant that they would no longer be a reproach to whomever saw them. They would no longer suffer embarrassment. They would dwell securely. Rebuilding the wall was a reminder that God was at work among them.

A parallel can again be drawn between these events and the Messianic movement. Just as they were a remnant of Israel, so are Messianic Jews the spiritual remnant of Israel. Messianic Jews are spiritual Israel, the Israel of God. They returned to the land, but they were living in a land without walls. The land was weak, small, and reproachful. Messianic congregations, with some exceptions, tend to be small. They are not impressive in appearance. They tend to grow at a slow pace.

Sometimes, people who are part of Messianic congregations wonder if God is really at work among them. They wonder if anything is really going to happen and look towards larger, more comfortable places to go. It takes a pioneering spirit to be part of a Messianic congregation.

It is significant that the remnant in the land began to work on the walls. Almost everyone set out to build up the walls of Jerusalem. It was Nehemiah's testimony of God's power and grace that made the people come together. He encouraged them in the Lord and they rallied behind him. They were not all skilled, but they all were builders. They were as diverse as any group could be. Just like Messianic Jews. They are not all seminary or even Bible school trained. They are not all teachers, artists or musicians. They come from a variety of backgrounds, yet God has called them together to be part of this movement. It means making congregations a high priority; giving of time, energy, and financial resources.

It involves the realization that the Messianic movement is not just another man-made institution, but is the work of God. Those who are part of Messianic congregations are involved in the restoration of an ancient movement. When they look at Messianic congregations, they do not see small, isolated congregations. They see themselves as part of something larger. They recognize that what God is doing in their congregation, He is also doing among Messianic congregations around the world. They realize they are the revival of the Messianic movement that existed in Jerusalem from the resurrection of Yeshua through the fourth century. They have returned from exile and are involved in building up the movement.

Some people question whether Messianic Judaism is the work of God because it faces opposition. In Nehemiah's time, Sanballat was angry when they began rebuilding. He ridiculed the builders and their work. He called them feeble, their task large, their attempts futile. What he pointed out was true. The task was enormous. The stones were weak. The city had been burned. The main building material, sandstone, was weakened by fire. Nehemiah prayed. It says that they rebuilt the wall until it reached half it's height. The people worked with all their hearts. Nehemiah encouraged the people, saying, *Don't be afraid. Remember the Lord who is Great and Awesome.*

Like these people, Messianic Jews in Messianic congregations also find opposition. Opposition comes from the Jewish community because of Messiah. They say the congregations are nothing. They say Messianic Jews are small and plain and the movement is fragile and will crumble.

Opposition from liberal churches comes because of how the Bible is believed. They say Messianic Jews should leave Jews alone, forgetting that they too need to meet their Messiah. Messianic Jews even get opposition from within. People say, "Don't do something because resources are limited," or "because it was never done this way before." They say, "Be careful to avoid all conflict."

Opposition from without or within erodes confidence. When these voices come the words of Nehemiah give comfort: *Don't be afraid of them. Remember the Lord, who is Great and Awesome.*

Nehemiah's wall was completed in fifty-two days. When the builders were finished, their enemies lost self-confidence, realizing that God was work. People sometimes look for the Lord to go before them so that they can hide behind Him and not face opposition. They think that if there is opposition that what they are doing must not be of God. The Lord's people need to stand their ground as they serve Him. They need to study His word, and when they know His will, press forward to accomplish it. If Nehemiah and the poeple of Israel had waited for an end to opposition, Jerusalem never would have been rebuilt. If Messianic Jews wait for an end to opposition, they will be waiting a very long time. The Lord has assigned a task. Messianic Jews must move forward.

CHAPTER TEN

THE ROLE OF GENTILES IN MESSIANIC CONGREGATIONS

There are many different reasons why Gentiles are attracted to and attend Messianic congregations, and it would be a terrible mistake to assume that all Gentiles attend for the same reason.

The subject of Gentiles in a Messianic Congregation is difficult to address. If a Messianic congregation has few or no Gentiles, or expresses itself in an exclusively Jewish religious and cultural framework, it is accused of putting up a "middle wall of partition." However, if the congregation has a higher proportion of non-Jews, or its worship style contains elements from both the non-Jewish *and* Jewish cultures, its authenticity as a Jewish congregation may be called into question.

The question that needs to be addressed is not how many Gentiles are too many. The real issue is what place Gentiles occupy in Messianic congregations. On one hand, some complain that Gentiles occupy a second-class position in the Messianic movement. On the other hand, since seventy to eighty-five percent of Messianic leaders are married to non-Jewish spouses, there has been a greater attempt on the part of the Messianic leadership to protect the status of Gentiles in Messianic congregations.

Those who feel that Gentiles are treated as second-class congregants are probably reacting to the dominant Jewish ethnic expression within the services, a culture with which the Gentile congregant may not be familiar. Since the Jewish culture is different from his own, he may confuse his lack of cultural association for a feeling of discrimination. While there may be some truth to the accusation that Gentiles occupy a second-class status in *some* congregations, more often than not, this is not the case. A Gentile that does not feel at home in a different culture would naturally feel a bit alienated, a feeling Jewish believers have had to deal with when entering the world of the Gentile church.

Many Gentiles make the error of thinking that their churches are culturally neutral. In reality, they reflect the culture of the predominant ethnic group within them, whether they be African-American, Latino, Anglo-Saxon or any other ethnic group. Messianic congregations are not practicing discrimination but are expressing their faith through their own Jewish culture, which is based upon the Scriptures. If it is discrimination for Messianic Jewish congregations to be Jewish, then it follows that non-Jewish oriented congregations are practicing discrimination by not being more Jewish in their worship style. Nevertheless, a Gentile with a correct attitude will adjust to cultural differences.

It's a shame that Messianic congregations, in an attempt to be sensitive to the Gentiles in their midst, have often tried to play down the Jewishness of their services, and in their attempt to be accommodating have lost sight of their own goals and vision as a Jewish congregation. It has been said in some quarters of the Messianic movement that the Messianic vision is the goal that "Jew and Gentile might become one." This a notion that may be attractive to those seeking to pacify Gentiles in the congregations, but it is not the Messianic vision of the Scriptures. The Messianic vision is the redemption of the Jewish people, not the amelioration of the Gentiles.

All Messianic congregations have non-Jewish members, and they occupy positions ranging from spectator/congregant to elder, or even leader of the congregation. The issue of "how far a Gentile can go" in a Messianic congregation is not based upon a caste system, but rather a person's heart attitude and spiritual gifts.

To begin to understand the role of Gentiles in Messianic

congregations, it is essential to recognize the various reasons why Gentiles are attracted to Messianic congregations. One congregant summed it up this way: "In a Messianic congregation, you have three kinds of people: first you have your Jewish believers; then you have your Gentiles who really love the Jews; then you have your Gentiles who come to watch the Jews dance." While more precise distinctions can and should be made, his observation was not without truth. Non-Jews attend Messianic congregations for a multitude of reasons. The following are the different categories of non-Jewish participants I have observed over the years.

The first group of Gentiles consists of those who are married to Jews. For this group, participation is an adjustment. However, it is easier for them than for other non-Jews because of the cultural connection through marriage, as well as through their children's Jewish heritage. This group of Gentiles may or may not view themselves as Jewish, but they do view themselves as connected to the Messianic congregation and to the Jewish people. This group tends to be supportive and loyal to the congregation and its vision. They believe that they occupy a legitimate place of service and can be found in virtually any role in the Messianic congregation.

The second group of Gentiles consists of "lovers of Israel." This group needs to be sub-divided into three categories. The first sub-category is made up of those that genuinely love the Jewish people and seek to befriend and reach out to them with the love of Yeshua. They believe that their place in the Messianic congregation is to build it up and strengthen it out of their love for the Jewish people and their desire to serve the Lord. Such people are an asset and a blessing to any congregation. As with the previous group, these people can be found in any number of positions, including eldership and congregational leadership.

The second sub-group is made up of those that say they "love" the Jews and want to help the Jewish people. However, the reason they "love" the Jews is not out of concern for the well-being of Jewish people, but rather out of a desire to receive a blessing for themselves. They believe God's promise to Abraham, in Genesis 12:3,

> *I will bless those who bless you, and whoever curses you I will curse; and all peoples on earth will be blessed through you.*

It is preferable for non-Jews to seek the well-being of the Jewish people rather than their harm. Nevertheless, relegating Jewish people to the status of a sacred "good luck charm" is not genuine love. These Gentiles eventually become offended when their good intentions go unappreciated by the Jewish people, and they usually leave the Messianic congregation, complaining about the ungratefulness of the people. This kind of "love" for Jews is not really love. The apostle Paul said, in 1 Corinthians 13:5, "It [love] is not self seeking." People that seek blessings for themselves by "blessing" the Jews are not motivated by love but by selfishness. Such a person is not capable of being a genuine blessing in a Messianic congregation.

The third sub-group is made up of those that have no special love for Jewish people, but rather have a love for Jewish things. These people are trying to become as Jewish as possible, rather than trying to reach Jewish people for Yeshua. They often claim to have a "family oral tradition" of Jewish ancestry, or in some cases, claim that "God revealed to them that they are Jewish." If they do manage to find a remote Jewish ancestor, even if it is a relation through marriage, they are inclined to treat other Gentiles as second-class citizens and try to be "more Jewish than the Jews." While Jewish believers rarely set up this type of caste system, Gentile believers that are trying to legitimatize themselves as Jews, are inclined to be critical of other Gentiles with a less impressive pedigree. They tend to be the most supportive of a more traditionally Jewish form of worship. They also tend to be hypercritical of Gentile-oriented churches, and tend to consider the Messianic congregation's worship style more theologically correct and more authentically biblical. Sooner or later such people become critical of the Messianic congregation because it is "not Jewish enough" for them. They tend to play out their participation and eventually leave, not having been of great long-term benefit to the congregation.

The third group of Gentiles consists of those that are neither lovers of the Jewish people nor of Jewish things. This type of person does not have romantic notions of Jewishness or an overwhelming concern for the Jewish people. This group of Gentiles attends a Messianic congregation in order to "keep the Jews in line." Their attitude is that they are in the congregation to teach the Jews how to be real "Christians," and they envision their role as protecting the Jewish believers from becoming "enslaved to the Law." They often accuse Messianic congregations of putting up a dividing wall between Jews and Gentiles, or of relegating Gentiles to the status of modern-day Gibeonite wood cutters and water carriers. These accusations are unfair and inaccurate. The fact is, non-Jews can, and in many cases do, occupy any available position in the congregation, including congregational leader. People that say such things do not really understand the *mechitza*, the "wall of partition." It has wrongly been called a "wall of division," or even a "wall of enmity." The *mechitza* was something that divided men and women in the temple, and is still in existence in Orthodox synagogues today. The reason it exists is as a sign of holiness. It was considered a holy thing for men and women to be separated in worship. Likewise, for Jews and pagans to be separated. When the apostle Paul referred to the wall of partition being broken down, he was not referring to a wall of difference or enmity, but to a wall that separated the holy from the profane. With the tearing down of this wall of partition, Gentiles that believed in Yeshua were no longer considered filthy pagans. Jews and Gentiles were now able to enjoy holy fellowship together in Yeshua. Jews could still be Jews and Gentiles could remain Gentiles, and they could fellowship as brothers even though they were different.

Apart from the fact that this view is both condescending and paternalistic, it also has anti-Semitic overtones. This view assumes that the Gospel of Yeshua is opposed to anything Jewish and that part of the Good News involves separating Jewish people from their own heritage. While in attendance at a Messianic congregation, this group of Gentiles asks for a "50-50" split, where equal time is given to "Christian" things. For example, Christian hymns get equal time with Messianic music; "Christian" holidays (e.g., Christmas and Easter) get equal time with

Jewish (biblical) holy days; and "Christian" terminology (e.g., Jesus Christ) gets equal time with Messianic Jewish terminology (e.g., *Yeshua ha Mashiach*). Such people do not last long in Messianic congregations because they are offended when their attitudes are not appreciated.

The fourth group of Gentiles consists of those disgruntled with the churches they came from. They attend a Messianic congregation because they have an anti-church attitude, and they think of Messianic congregations as being anti-church. This viewpoint involves a serious misunderstanding of what the Messianic movement is all about. When these Gentiles discover that Messianic is not synonymous with anti-church, they usually leave. Such people are not really wanted by Messianic congregations because a solid congregation cannot be built on bitterness and criticism.

It is clear that not everyone is called to a Messianic congregation. It can be safely said that among the key elements that constitute a calling to a Messianic congregation are: a love for Jewish people that manifests itself in service, not a desire for appreciation; a desire to see the congregation grow in its cultural context; and a desire to see the congregation grow in the number of Jewish people coming to know the Messiah.

If it is kept in mind that the purpose of a Messianic congregation is to minister and reach out to Jewish people, it becomes apparent that Gentiles who desire to help build the congregation will find a home there, and be equal members with Jewish believers. However, a Gentile that is only interested in satisfying his own ego or trying to be something he is not will not feel at home.

A final question to ask is, what should the attitude of the Messianic congregation be towards the Gentiles in its midst? Rather than being condescending and having a monolithic approach, most congregations rightly examine each person, one at a time, whether Jew or Gentile. If a person has a humble spiritual attitude, they will be welcomed by the congregation. However, if they come with an unhealthy attitude, they will eventually either change their attitude or leave.

Finding One's Place in a Messianic Congregation

A more practical side to this issue is "how do I as a non-Jew find my place in the Messianic congregation I am attending?" This section will present some general guidelines. Everyone has different experiences, but these guidelines will make fitting-in easier.

First, when a Gentile attends a Messianic congregation, he should look for those aspects of the service he already understands and should seek to relate wherever possible. He should take notes on things that he does not understand, and ask if there is literature available explaining the Messianic perspective (this book for example). During the fellowship time, he should introduce himself to one of the elders or to the leader of the congregation. The leader is usually surrounded by people that want to speak to him immediately after the service. Thus, it is best to ask if there is a better time to call or meet for the purpose of asking questions about the service.

Second, one should not come with an attitude and checklist that will be critical of the service. Remember, it is a different culture with a different worship style from traditional churches. It would be as unfair to judge one's church by Messianic standards as it is to judge a Messianic congregation by church standards. One should look for things common to both traditions and feel connected to them. Gentiles should strive to find out the meaning of things they do not understand, not for the purpose of criticism, but for the purpose of gaining new understanding and spiritual insight, and finding new ways to connect in the congregation.

Third, be patient. It takes time to learn new ways. One should invest his time to learn Jewish traditions and manner of worship. It will take a little while, but it is worth it. This involves actually practicing the Jewish traditions and participating in the worship service. Otherwise, one cannot expect to connect with the congregation.

Fourth, come in humility, but not apologetically. Come with a desire to learn, but do not apologize for being a Gentile. God created you as such, and Messianic congregations are not anti-

Gentile. Respect whatever God made you, but it takes humility to learn and fit in.

Fifth, do not call yourself a Jew if you are not. This is not an issue of social class, but honesty. A frequent accusation leveled against the Messianic community is that it is really a Christian movement camouflaged to look Jewish. If Gentiles are calling themselves Messianic Jews, but do not look Jewish or relate as Jews do, it sends a message that the movement is false. Gentiles do not need to call themselves Messianic Jews to fully participate in the services and be full members of their congregation. The term Messianic *believer* is more accurate and preferable for them to use.

Following these general guidelines will help people find their place as they begin to recognize their spiritual gifts and calling. Regardless, Gentiles are welcome in the Messianic movement, and it is the hope and prayer of this author that they will be very blessed and will also be a great blessing to Jewish believers.

CONCLUSION

As you have read, since the first century, there has been a remnant of Jewish believers in the Messiah. In its early stages, the Messianic faith began and developed within its native Jewish context. If a Jewish person embraced Yeshua, his identity as a Jew would not have been called into question or repressed. As Luke records in Acts 21:20,

> *Then they said to Paul, You see, brother, how many thousands of Jews have believed, and all of them are zealous for the law.*

Jewishness and belief that Yeshua was the Messiah was a natural relationship that blended perfectly. In subsequent history, Pharisaic Judaism displaced most other Jewish forms and became normative. It condemned Messianic Judaism (as well as other groups) as unacceptable. At the same time, the developing Church became predominantly Gentile and, after the destruction of Jerusalem, the Gentile influence, seeking uniformity in its own context, caused the Messianic faith to be further removed from its Jewish origin. Later history saw the Church commit anti-Semitic acts against Jewish people in the name of Jesus. This hatred and violence, coupled with the cultural and religious forces within and without of the Jewish community, caused Jewish people to look upon faith in Yeshua, their promised Messiah, as a non-Jewish religion. Jewish people who came to believe in Yeshua as Messiah were considered traitors and heretics by the Jewish community. Faith in the Messiah and being Jewish were seen as mutually exclusive. For the most part,

Jewish people ceased to consider the Messiahship of Yeshua for themselves.

With the advent of the Messianic congregational movement, Jewish believers began to identify themselves once again as Jews. They sought to stand together as a united witness to their own people, declaring that it is possible to be Jewish and believe in Yeshua. The Messianic congregational movement is a nineteenth/twentieth century phenomenon which parallels the re-establishment of the modern State of Israel.

The Messianic movement is young, yet it has an ancient heritage. Because of its youth, the movement is in many ways a pioneer movement, blazing new trails as well as some which have not been traveled for over 1,500 years. While there are some clear distinctions between this movement and traditional Christianity, there are also some important similarities. This new movement can learn from these. It must take care that, in the name of contextualization, it does not throw out the good with the bad.

In these latter days, history appears to be coming around full-circle. Yeshua appeared while the nation of Israel existed and the Jewish people lived in the land. The good news went out from the Jewish people to the nations of the world. Subsequent events turned Jewish people away from Yeshua and crushed the Messianic movement. Jewish people were scattered all over the globe. The national entity of Israel disappeared.

As the return of the Messiah approaches, Jewish people are back in the land. Israel is once again a national entity. Jewish people are believing in Yeshua. Believers, both Jewish and non-Jewish, need to stand with the Messianic movement, as one in the Messiah.

Jewish believers of the first century looked for Yeshua's return and for the redemption of the Jewish people. So do modern-day Jewish believers. Messianic Jews often express the heart of an early Messianic Jew:

> *Brothers, my heart's deepest desire and*
> *my prayer to God for Israel*
> *is for their salvation*
> (Romans 10:1).

APPENDIX ONE
MESSIANIC CONGREGATION SURVEY ANALYSIS

In conducting this survey, I chose to poll those leaders whose congregations have been in existence for more than one year and have more than ten members, be they Jewish or Gentile. My purpose in setting this survey criteria was that I wanted to measure factors in those congregations which are more or less substantially developed and are truly representative of the Messianic congregational movement. Those congregations which have been in existence for less than one year would not have enough of a track record for me to be able to glean meaningful results for the purposes of this survey. Those with fewer than ten members are too small to be considered a congregation for the purposes of this study. Such congregations fall into the category of a home group bible study, from which many of the present day congregations grew. The UMJC criterion for a full-member congregation is that the congregation must have at least ten Messianic Jewish members. A list of congregations participating in this survey is contained in Appendix Two.

In this survey, I sought to measure those practices, factors, and events which are typical in Messianic congregations. The data from this survey reflects the perceptions of the leaders of Messianic congregations of the Messianic movement and should be of assistance to those congregations which are seeking to become established.

This survey was conducted during the MJAA Messiah '87 Conference in Grantham, Pennsylvania in July 1987, and during the UMJC Conference in Atlanta, Georgia in August 1987, and administered by mail to members of the FMC during September 1987. Questionnaires were mailed to each FMC congregation and were returned promptly.

The procedure followed was to approach each congregational leader personally, requesting him to fill out the questionnaire. Most questionnaires were received before the end of each conference. Several were returned by mail. Thirty six congregations took part in the survey. Two were excluded because they failed to meet the criteria for the survey because of their size or age. Four leaders expressed their desire to help but disliked filling out questionnaires, especially one this long.

After tabulating the survey results, a copy of the data was returned to each leader with a self-addressed, stamped envelope and a post test requesting they respond to the results of the survey and return their response. An analysis of the data follows. The total number of congregations participating was 30 (N=30).

Table 1: Date Congregation was Formed

Years	#	%
1985–1987	2	7
1980–1984	14	46
1975–1979	8	27
1970–1974	3	10
Pre-1970	3	10

These figures indicate the majority of Messianic congregations have come into being in the past decade, the majority between 1975–1984. This reflects the newness of the Messianic congregational movement and the upsurge of Messianic Jewish expression over Hebrew Christian expression, as manifested in the Hebrew Christian/Messianic Jewish Alliance of America conference in 1975.[1]

Table 2: Years Spiritual Leader in the Congregation

Years	#	%
0–3	6	20
4–5	7	23
6–8	10	33
9–12	5	17
12+	2	7

Comparing the ages of the congregations with the length of time the Spiritual Leader has been in the congregation, the data indicates a low pastoral turnover rate. This may be the result of several factors. First, leading a Messianic congregation is a somewhat specialized occupation. There may not be many people qualified to fill leadership positions. Second, some of the congregations are led by the men who founded them, making their continuing presence more secure. Because most of these congregations are so young, it is hard to draw concrete conclusions about pastoral longevity. More time is needed to see which factors may affect the duration of Messianic pastoral ministry.

Of the Spiritual Leaders polled, twenty-seven were married and three were single. Those who were single indicated that they were interested in marriage if they were to find the right person.

Table 3: Age of Spiritual Leader

Age	#	%
26–30	3	10
31–35	6	20
36–40	11	37
41–45	4	13
46–50	2	7
51–60	4	13

The age of most of the leaders in Messianic congregations ranged between thirty-one and forty-five with the highest percentage between thirty-six and forty. Again, this may be reflecting the relative youth of the movement in general. Of the six largest congregations, the youngest leader is thirty-five and the oldest is fifty-two. This would seem to have no bearing on the size and growth of a congregation.

Of the four smallest congregations, the spiritual leaders range in age between thirty-one and forty-four. It would appear that the age of the congregational leader is of little or no consequence in regards to congregational size and growth.

Table 4: Educational Background of Spiritual Leader

Degree	#	%
Undergraduate	28	93
Master of Divinity	14	47
Masters (secular)	8	27
Bible College	10	33
Post Graduate	5	17
Informal Education	2	7

These figures should be interpreted in light of the age of the Messianic movement. Forty-seven percent of Spiritual Leaders have earned Masters of Divinity degrees.

Of the leaders of the six largest congregations, four have Masters of Divinity degrees or the equivalent, and two are Bible college graduates. Of the four smallest congregations, two have seminary education, one Bible school education, and one no formal Bible training. This would seem to indicate that some formal Bible training may be helpful in growing a healthy congregation, but probably does not affect the size of the congregation. While education is not the foremost emphasis, it is valued and encouraged. The UMJC has a Yeshiva (Bible School) for pastoral training. Recently the Messiah Bible Institute has been organized for basic and graduate theological studies in the Washington D.C. area and the MJAA has begun a leadership training program as well. Education, being highly valued in Jewish culture, may also account for the high undergraduate percentage.

Table 5: Spiritual Leader's Religious Upbringing

Branch	#	%
Jewish		
Orthodox	9	30
Conservative	7	23
Reform	4	13
Secular	6	20
Messianic	3	10
Non-Jewish	1	4

Most Messianic leaders are from Jewish backgrounds of the more traditional type. The percentage of leaders from traditional

(Orthodox/Conservative) backgrounds is inverted with the percentage of traditional households in the Jewish community. In the Jewish community at large, Reform/secular households represent the largest percentage, and Orthodox the smallest. It could be that the Orthodox/Conservative emphasis on God in their upbringing may have contributed to these leaders becoming believers. It is also interesting that ten percent of the Messianic leaders polled come from a Messianic background. According to question 1, ten percent of Messianic congregations were formed prior to 1970, which indicates that some leadership has come as the fruit of the early Messianic congregational plantings.

Table 6: Spiritual Leader's Theological Orientations (Most surveyed had several)

Orientation	#	%
Charismatic	23	77
Non-Charismatic	5	17
Dispensational	8	27
Covenant	2	7
Promise	7	23
Pre-Tribulation	13	43
Mid-Tribulation	1	3
Post-Tribulation	2	7
Pre-Millennial	17	57

Table 7: Congregation's Agreement With Spiritual Leader's Theological Position

Agreement	#	%
Fully	26	87
Partially	4	13

Although seventy-seven percent of spiritual leaders label themselves charismatic in orientation, Table 24 indicates that only seventeen percent of them consider the exercise of spiritual gifts a major part of their services. Sixty percent consider it minor. This suggests that while the leaders want to identify with God's gifts, power, and blessing, their praxis is for the most part minor on the charismatic issue. This, combined with the results of Table 7, reflects that the issue of charismatic expression is a gray area in many Messianic congregations, unlike many non-Jewish congregations which have sharp lines drawn delineating charismatic or non-charismatic orientation. One reason why Messianic congregations are less precise on this issue may be that these congregations see themselves as first and foremost Messianic, not charismatic and non-charismatic. They do not want to exclude brothers of other views especially since the Messianic pool is small. Among the six largest congregations, four of the six are charismatic, and two of the four place major emphasis on the exercise of spiritual gifts in their services. Of the four smallest congregations, three of the four have a charismatic orientation. Compared with the larger congregations, this would seem to indicate that charismatic expression is not a major factor in congregational growth.

Another possible reason for the variety of views in the congregations may be that most congregational members have come out of the dispersion of various denominations bringing with them the views they held in those groups.

129

Table 8: Spiritual Leaders Primary Preaching Style

Preaching Style	#	%
Expositional	24	80
Bible Study	4	13
Follow Prescribed Texts [i.e., Torah, Haftorah readings]	4	13
Topical-Textual	16	53

The leaders were permitted to respond to more than one description of their teaching style. Most Messianic leaders preach expositionally, overlapping with topical messages. This emphasis may reflect Jewish believers coming to the Lord because of the testimony of scripture, not because it was something they grew up with (except those from Messianic backgrounds). The Word of God is primary in Messianic congregations because it, and not tradition or upbringing, is the basis of the Messianic faith in Yeshua.

Four of the spiritual leaders of the six largest congregations reported their preaching style to be mainly expositional, while two classified their style to be mainly textual/topical. All of the four smallest congregations have expositional preaching as their primary preaching emphasis. It would appear that no significant conclusions that might impact on congregational growth can be drawn from the preaching styles of the larger congregations in comparison to the others.

Table 9: Style of the Congregation's Government

Government	#	%
Eldership	21	70
Congregational	2	7
Pastoral	7	23

Most congregations follow an eldership form of government comprised of an equal plurality of elders or elders with the pastor as head. Twenty-three percent follow a strong pastoral model, with only two congregations following the congregational model. Reasons for these models may be biblical patterns or influence from outside the movement (denominational backgrounds and affiliations).

Of the six largest congregations, all are governed by elders. This compares with the smaller congregations where three of the four are governed by elders, while one follows the pastoral model. This would imply that the type of government has no effect on congregational size or growth.

Table 10: Leadership Positions Held by Women in the Congregation

Office	**#**	**%**
Pastor/Messianic Rabbi	0	0
Worship Leader/Cantor	4	13
Elder	2	7
Shammash/Deacon	11	37
Trustee	2	7

None of the Messianic congregations have women in a pastoral role, but many allow women in other leadership positions. Of the two congregations that had women in eldership positions, one is affiliated with the Presbyterian Church-USA and the other with the Assemblies of God, both of which allow female elders. Another congregation did not have single women elders but followed the practice of having elder couples where both husband and wife had to meet the criteria for eldership and minister as a team. The most common area of leadership open to women in the Messianic congregations is Shammash, a more service-oriented rather than authority-oriented position. The role of women in Messianic congregations, as in other congregations is in a state of flux. They may never go beyond the position of Shammash, or they may very well be involved in some type of pastoral role. The fact is, Scripture does teach that women should not be in authority over a man; yet, it is true that in many situations a woman can minister in a place where a man cannot. In such situations, we may eventually see women on a pastoral team working under the leadership and authority of a male spiritual leader.

Table 11: Percentage of Membership from a Jewish Background

% of Members	#	%
1–25%	1	3
25–50%	11	37
51–75%	17	57
76–100%	1	3

Most Messianic congregations that participated in this survey have percentages of Jewish membership between twenty-five and fifty percent. This illustrates that Messianic congregations are not putting up a "middle wall of partition" between Jewish and non-Jewish people. Both are equally members of these congregations.

The larger congregations average between fifty to seventy-five percent of their membership being Jewish. In the smaller congregations, three averaged between fifty and seventy-five percent, and one between seventy-five and one hundred percent Jewish.

Table 12: Percentage of Marriages Involving Intermarriage

% of Members	#	%
1–25%	6	20
25–50%	10	33
51–75%	10	33
76–100%	3	10
No response	4	13

As with membership, the majority of congregations have between twenty-five to seventy-five percent intermarriage. As a whole, the smaller congregations had a lower rate overall in intermarriage than the larger congregations. While the difference is slight, and more data is needed to draw more accurate conclusions, we can infer from the data that congregations which exhibit a greater openness to intermarried couples will attract more such couples. This may be a contributing factor for congregational growth. Two factors are of significance: First, Messianic congregations provide an ideal situation for intermarried couples because of the Jewish cultural emphasis as well as New Testament faith. Secondly, because of this dual emphasis, Messianic congregations are in a strong position to reach out to unbelieving intermarried and potentially intermarried couples.

Table 13: Congregations with Formal Membership

# of Congregations:	23
%	77

Twenty three congregations have formal membership. This represents seventy-seven percent of those polled. Five of the six largest congregations have formal membership. Of the four smallest congregations, two have formal membership and two do not. One of the two which does not have formal membership has indicated they are moving in the direction of having it. Formal membership may be a factor which influences congregational growth. It defines boundaries pertaining to the congregation and calls attendees to greater commitment. From the data, this can only be conjectured. More research would be needed to draw solid conclusions.

Table 14: Average Attendance at Main Weekly Worship Service

Attendance	#	%
10–25	4	13
26–50	11	37
51–75	6	20
76–100	3	10
101–150	3	10
151–250	2	7
250+	1	3

The size of the average Messianic congregation is between 26–100 people. While it should be noted that four larger Messianic congregations declined to participate in the survey, the bulk of the congregations are still in this 26–100 size category. This average size may be affected by the age of the currently emerging Messianic movement, but also points to the absence of many Jewish believers who are still in traditional churches. This movement is still in a pioneering stage, and as Jews in Israel long for those in the dispersion to return home, so do Messianic Jews look to Jewish believers in churches to *make aliyah,* to return to their people, culture, and heritage in Messianic congregations.

From the data in Appendix One, comparing size and age (Tables 1 and 14), it appears that age does not have a significant effect upon the size of Messianic congregations. The largest congregations are between six and fifteen years old, with the exception of one congregation which is fifty four years old. There are other congregations which are older, yet smaller.

There are other factors which must affect the size of the congregation. Among them would be the Jewish population of the vicinity in which the congregation is located. All of the cities which have congregations with over one hundred members are cities with significantly large Jewish populations. Other factors may be the presence of other Messianic congregations in the same city.

Table 15: Number of weekly services

# of Weekly Services	#	%
1	15	50
2	14	47
3	1	3

Table 16: Day of main worship service

Day	#	%
Friday	16	53
Saturday	13	43
Sunday	12	40

note: 11 of the 12 congregations meeting on Sunday also had Friday or Saturday services as well.

The bulk of these services take place on Friday evenings or Saturday mornings. Most had Friday/Saturday, or Friday/Sunday services. Only one had Friday, Saturday, Sunday services, but they have since discontinued their Saturday morning services. Four congregations listed Sunday as their main worship service. The reason for the Friday/Saturday emphasis instead of Sunday as primary may be two fold: first, Friday/Saturday is a traditional Jewish day of worship honoring the Shabbat, and He who is Lord of Shabbat; secondly, forty percent of Messianic congregations meet in church buildings whose congregations occupy their buildings on Sundays (see Table 24).

Of the six largest congregations, four meet on Saturday mornings only, one Friday evening and Sunday, and one on Sunday morning only. Of the smallest congregations, three meet on Saturday mornings and one on Friday evening. It would appear that day of the main service is not a major factor in congregational size and growth. One of the mid-size congregations indicated a loss of attendance when they moved their services from Friday evenings to Saturday mornings.

Table 17: Congregations with Special Services for Jewish Holidays

Holiday	#	%
Rosh HaShana	30	100
Yom Kippur	30	100
Passover	30	100
Hanukkah	29	97
Purim	29	97
Sukkot	29	97
Shavuot	23	76
Simchat Torah	20	67
Israel Independence Day	11	37
Yom HaShoah	10	33
T'shi'b'Av	5	17
Lag'b'omer	1	3

Most Messianic congregations celebrate the major Jewish holidays with the relatively minor holidays being shown less attention. This may be for two reasons. First, Messianic Jews celebrate Jewish holidays to present the Messiah's foreshadowing in them. Those holidays not emphasized may not carry any dominant Messianic themes. Second, these holidays are celebrated as a point of cultural identification. If they are not strongly emphasized by the Jewish community, the Messianic community may not be motivated to celebrate them either. An exception to this would be the innovation by some Messianic congregations to celebrate first fruits, a biblical holiday not celebrated by the Jewish community.

Table 18: Congregations that Observe These Holidays

Holiday	#	%
Yeshua's Birth	14	47
(2 in conjunction w/ Sukkot)		
Yeshua's Resurrection	20	67
(5 in conjunction w/ First Fruits)		

There is a hesitancy among some Messianic congregations to celebrate Yeshua's birth and resurrection. One reason may be that they are viewed as non-Jewish. It could be argued that since the Messiah is Jewish, Messianic believers should not refrain from celebrating these holy days. But some Messianic congregations may refrain from these holidays as a matter of cultural sensitivity to the Jewish people.

Christmas and Easter represent very difficult times of the year for Jewish people, because at no other times are they more aware of their being different from the general populous. It can be traumatic for Jewish children to not participate in elaborate holiday festivities Gentile children celebrate. To do so would seem to celebrate a non-Jewish holiday and a breach of

Jewishness. It can be harder on parents knowing they must deny their children from participating in an obviously enjoyable festivity, while trying to emphasize the blessing of being Jewish. Another possible reason some Messianic congregations do not celebrate these holidays is the commercialism that accompanies both Christmas and Easter. It is for this reason that a small percentage of Messianic congregations have begun to celebrate Messiah's birth and resurrection in conjunction with existing Jewish holidays. Sukkot (Tabernacles), the Feast of Booths, is a reminder that through the wilderness wanderings in the desert, God was indeed with them. Zechariah 14 teaches that the Lord will come and reign from Jerusalem, and the world will come year after year to celebrate the Feast of Tabernacles. Tabernacles is associated with God dwelling among us. John 1:14 says, "and the Word became flesh and dwelt among us." Others claim that His birth should be celebrated on the 25th of *Kislev,* which is the first day of *Chanukah.* This date corresponds to December 25th, and as the first night of Chanukah, the festival of lights, Yeshua's birth is called to mind because Yeshua is the light of the world.

Yeshua's resurrection is commemorated by some congregations in conjunction with *Bikkurim,* First Fruits, because Yeshua is the first fruits of the resurrection.

Table 19: Elements of Jewish Tradition and Liturgy in the Worship Service.

Element	#	%
Kipah	24	80
Kiddush	24	80
Tallit	21	70
Traditional Prayers	21	70
Shabbat Candles	20	67
T'fillin	4	13

Among the elements of Jewish tradition used in Messianic congregations, the Kipah (head covering) and Kiddush (blessing over the wine and bread) are the most common, followed by the usage of some traditional prayers and the wearing of Tallit (prayer shawl). It could be assumed that the figures concerning the kindling of Shabbat candles would have been higher if more congregations worshipped on Friday evenings when they are normally lit. If the percentage of those kindling Shabbat candles is compared with those having Friday services, it can be seen that all Friday evening congregations kindle the candles. Several Saturday morning congregations noted that their people light candles at home on Friday evenings.

Table 20: What Percentage of Male Congregants Wear

	Degree	#	%
Kipah			
	All	0	0
	Most	11	37
	Some	14	47
	None	5	17
Tallit	**Degree**	**#**	**%**
	All	0	0
	Most	2	7
	Some	18	60
	None	10	33
T'fillin	**Degree**	**#**	**%**
(Phylacteries)	All	0	0
	Most	0	0
	Some	5	17
	None	25	83

Table 21: Congregations that Supply Kipot & Tallit

Supplied	#	%
Kipah	17	57
Tallit	4	14

Table 22: Percentage of Male Leadership Wearing

Kipah	Degree	#	%
	All	10	33
	Most	10	33
	Some	4	14
	None	6	20
Tallit	Degree	#	%
	All	3	10
	Most	7	23
	Some	11	37
	None	9	30
T'fillin (Phylacteries)	Degree	#	%
	All	0	
	Most	0	
	Some	4	14
	None	26	86

These figures suggest that the kipah followed by the tallit is the most commonly used religious article worn in the congregations. Laying t'fillin is mostly practiced by Orthodox Jews and certainly not by many Messianic congregations.

Table 23: Congregations with a Torah

#	%
10	33

Table 23A: Congregations where Torah is used in Service

Amount	#	%
Frequently	7	23
Occasionally	3	10

One third of surveyed Messianic congregations have Torahs. One reason the other two thirds do not may be the high cost of purchasing a Torah. Among those congregations that have a Torah, there is a higher percentage of those who wear Kipah and Tallit. Having a more traditional Torah service may account for a more traditional use of kipah, tallit, and liturgy. Four of the six larger congregations have Torah scrolls. Two of the four smaller congregations have Torah scrolls. The possession and use of a Torah would seem to have no statistical value in determining congregational size or growth.

Table 24: Part Played by the Following in the Worship Services

Exercise of Spiritual Gifts	Degree	#	%
	Major	5	17
	Minor	18	60
	None	7	23

Traditional Liturgy	Degree	#	%
	Major	8	27
	Minor	19	63
	None	3	10

Proclamation of the Word	Degree	#	%
	Major	27	90
	Minor	3	10
	None	0	0

Music	Degree	#	%
	Major	27	90
	Minor	2	7
	None	0	0

Other aspects of the worship listed were sharing, testimonies, prayer, fellowship, and children's time.

Table 25: Kind of Music Ministry of Congregation:

Kind	#	%
Singing	27	90
Instruments	26	87
Dance	9	30

From this data, we see the major emphases in Messianic worship clearly are Word proclamation and music. Of secondary emphasis are liturgy and exercise of spiritual gifts. This seems to indicate that the average Messianic congregation is a Word proclaiming congregation with a strong emphasis on music. Spiritual gifts and liturgy are part of the service, but neither are of central emphasis or primary importance.

Of the six major congregations, two listed exercise of spiritual gifts as a major emphasis, three as minor, and one as none. Two indicated a major emphasis on liturgy, three had a minor emphasis, and one had none. Five indicated a major emphasis on Preaching the Word and music, while one put a minor emphasis on each. This would support the conclusion that proclamation of the Word and music are the main elements of Messianic worship. Of the four smallest congregations, all put major emphases upon Word proclamation and music.

The music ministry of most congregations is limited to singing and playing various instruments. Some have dance ministries. Four of the six largest congregations have dance as an element in their music ministry. In light of the importance of the music ministry, it would make sense for Messianic congregations to build their music ministries.

Table 26: Type of Building in which Congregation Meets

Type of Facility	#	%
Home	1	3
Church	12	40
Leased facility/full time	4	13
Leased facility/part time	2	7
School	3	10
Own building	7	23
Lodge	1	3

The single most common facility in which Messianic congregations worship is a church building. Sixty percent of congregations meet elsewhere. Of the six largest congregations, two meet in schools (one is in the process of building its own facility), two meet in churches, one has its own building, and one leases a facility full time. Church buildings often can be used at a lesser cost especially if the church is sympathetic to the cause of the Messianic movement. There are two primary drawbacks involved in using a church building. First, in scheduling of services (i.e., Sundays are not practical). The second is the problem of the Messianic congregation being too closely identified with the ministry of that church. Such identification may be counterproductive to its witness to the Jewish community and to the congregation's own self identity.

Table 27: Congregations with a Hebrew/Shabbat School

#	%
22	73

Grade	#	%
Nursery	20	67
3–6	20	67
7–10	16	53
11–13	12	40
13–Adult	7	23

Messianic groups have been developing their own educational curricula for their education departments. Until recently, they have had to adapt materials from outside the movement. As the materials increase in various age groups, so too will there be Shabbat school classes beyond these groups.

Table 28: Congregations Affiliated with a Denomination Outside the Messianic movement:

#	%
7	23

#	Denomination
1	Evangelical Free Church of America
1	North American Baptist
1	Presbyterian Church in the USA
2	Assemblies of God
2	Other

Table 29: Congregations Affiliated with Messianic Groups

Group	#	%
UMJC	19	63
FMC	6	20
IAMCS/MJAA	9	30

note: several organizations are affiliated with more than one organization.

Most Messianic congregations are not affiliated with outside denominations. Those who are have either been planted by those denominations or in some way financially helped by them. Three of the largest congregations are affiliated in some way with outside denominations: one with Assemblies of God, one with Evangelical Free Church, and one with Presbyterian Church-USA. Almost all Messianic congregations belong to at least one of the three Messianic congregational organizations, with some belonging to more than one. Of the three organizations, one is oriented towards non-charismatic congregations, while the other two seek to be broad umbrella organizations. Among the reasons for being part of these organizations is the need for fellowship with those in a similar ministry and vision. Also it enables the movement to have a greater impact, speaking with a combined voice to issues affecting those in Messianic congregations.

Table 30: Congregations that Have Offerings in Worship Services

#	%
13	43

Table 30A: Congregations that Use a Tsadakah (charity) Box for Giving

#	%
17	57

Table 31: Extent Spiritual Leader is Financially Supported by the Congregation

Degree	#	%
Mostly	9	30
Partially	19	63
Not at all	2	7

From these figures it could be assumed that those who take up offerings are able to fully support their Spiritual Leader, while those with the Tsadakah box cannot. Contrary to this assumption, only eight of those congregations taking up offerings can fully support their Spiritual Leaders. This indicates that factors other than method of receiving offerings account for the congregation's ability to support the Spiritual Leader.

Table 32: Percentage of Congregation's Neighborhood that is Jewish

Degree	#	%
Mostly	9	30
Partially	19	63
Not al all	2	7

Table 33: Jewish Community in which Congregation is *Primarily* Situated

Identification	#	%
Orthodox	4	13
Conservative	9	30
Reform	11	37
Agnostic	1	3
Secular	5	17

Table 34: Spiritual Leader's Perception of the Jewish Community's Reaction to the Congregation's Presence

Reaction	**#**	**%**
Indifferent	16	53
Unaware of its existence	1	3
Part of the community	0	0
Antagonistic	12	40
Openly hostile	1	3

Most Messianic congregations are located in areas that are partly Jewish, as opposed to being located in the center of a Jewish neighborhood. One reason for this may be the changing demographics of Jewish communities where people no longer live in areas that are all one ethnic type or another. Most of the Jewish communities are predominantly conservative or reformed, reflecting the demographics of the average Jewish community.

The Spiritual Leaders perceive the Jewish reaction to the Messianic congregation as either indifferent or antagonistic. Some of the Spiritual Leaders commented that the average Jewish person was indifferent and curious, while the leaders of the community and anti-missionaries stir up hostility toward Messianic congregations.

Table 35: Number of Visitors Congregation Has in an Average Month

Visitors	**#**	**%**
1–4	2	7
5–10	12	40
11–20	11	37
20+	5	17

Table 36: Number of Visitors who are Jewish

Jewish Visitors	#	%
1–4	18	60
5–10	12	40
11–20	0	0
20+	0	0

Table 37: Number of Visitors who Return

Returning Visitors	#	%
1–4	24	80
5–10	6	20
11–20	0	0
20+	0	0

Most congregations average between five to twenty visitors per month. Of these, at least one and as many as ten may be Jewish. Eighty percent of the congregations have one to four visitors return. Twenty percent have as many as ten return. This indicates that the Messianic congregations are attracting both Jewish and non-Jewish people, and some visitors are returning. This indicates a healthy potential for growth.

Table 38: Congregation's Self-perception in Effectively Reaching the Unsaved Relatives of its Members

Effectiveness	#	%
Mostly	2	7
Somewhat	14	47
Slightly	11	37
Not Effective	3	10

The congregations see themselves as somewhat effective in reaching the unsaved relatives of their members. This may be because Messianic congregations are able to communicate that Jewish identity is sustained when a Jewish person believes in Yeshua.

Table 39: Activities of the Congregation Toward Outreach into the Community

Activity	#	%
Holiday Celebrations	22	73
Friendships	20	67
Literature Distribution	15	50
Advertising	15	50
Special Activities	15	50
Musical Presentations	13	43

Other outreach activities include: door to door; Evangelism Explosion; coffee houses; campus outreach; dance ministry, nursing home ministry, homeless outreach.

Table 40: Activities that Have Been the Most Successful in Making New Contacts and in Sharing Their Faith

Activity	#	%
Friendships	16	53
Holiday Celebrations	13	43
Special Activities	9	30
Advertising	6	20
Musical Presentations	6	20
Literature Distribution	2	7

Table 41: Outreach Methods which the Congregation is Most Comfortable With

Activity	#	%
Friendships	17	57
Holiday Celebrations	16	53
Special Activities	9	30
Advertising	8	27
Musical Presentations	6	20
Literature Distribution	1	3

While Messianic congregations utilize a plethora of methods for outreach, clearly friendship evangelism and holiday celebrations are the most effective methods of outreach. This suggests that holiday celebrations should be geared more to evangelism and people should be bolder in stepping out in sharing the Messiah with their friends.

Table 42: Average Attendance in Main Worship Services

Year	20-30	31-45	46-65	66-100	100-200	200+
1987	7	6	7	5	3	1
1986	7	8	5	6	2	1
1985	12	6	3	3	3	0
1984	12	5	3	2	3	0

Most congregations indicated growth over the past four years, with the exception of one who changed its worship day and another which had endured a split.

Table 43: Factors Attributed to Growth of Congregations by Their Leaders

Other factors of growth listed by congregational leaders included evangelism, publicity, worship style, move to larger facility, the Lord, The Word being proclaimed, word of mouth, prayer, planning for growth, opportunities for service, unity, grace.

One congregation indicated a decline in attendance as the result of moving worship from Sunday to Saturday.

In areas of outreach, the six largest polled congregations responded to the survey as follows:

Table 44A: Activities of the Congregation Toward Outreach into the Community

Activity	**#**
Holiday Celebrations	5
Friendships	2
Literature Distribution	3
Advertising	3
Special Activities	5
Musical Presentations	3

Table 44B: Activities that Have Been the Most Successful Making New Contacts, and Sharing Their Faith

Activity	**#**
Friendships	2
Holiday Celebrations	2
Special Activities	4
Musical Presentations	1

Table 44C: Outreach Method with Which the Congregation is Most Comfortable

Activity	#
Friendships	4
Holiday Celebrations	2
Special Activities	5
Musical Presentations	2
Evangelism Explosion	1

It would appear from these figures that the largest congregations see special activities as the most successful approach to outreach, along with friendship evangelism and holiday celebrations. Of the smaller congregations, friendship evangelism is the most popular outreach, followed by holiday and musical presentations. This would indicate that there is more to congregational growth than specific activities. In regards to congregational growth, Andrew Shishkoff, Spiritual Leader of Beth Messiah, Rockville, Md., (one of the largest congregations, doubled in size over the past four years) listed the following factors in his congregation's growth.

"The growth of our congregation is a result of the following factors plus others I'm sure that I'm not aware of or am forgetting.

1. Believing prayer. We began praying earnestly for growth as a leadership core five years ago. Continued prayer.

2. We set numerical goals for growth and spoke of those goals in an expectant way.

3. Vision for growth was communicated to the congregation. As leaders we conveyed our enthusiastic conviction that God intended to multiply our numbers.

4. Outside prophetic input. Men of God from outside the movement ministered faith and vision for growth to us.

5. A philosophy of maximum congregational participation and commitment to training new leaders. Growth demands that current members be *active*.

6. Planning for growth. Moving into larger facility. Start building fund. Improving graphic publications, improving sound equipment. Recruiting Shabbat School teachers, etc."

Of the larger congregations, four of the six have increased between fifty and one hundred percent over the past four years. While he did not speak for the other congregations, Shishkoff indicated that in the case of his congregation, growth was not the result of special activities and outreach attempts alone, but primarily involved prayer, intentional planning with goals, seeking to expand the congregation's vision for growth, seeking to motivate and maximize congregational participation and commitment in service to the congregation, and improving the quality of the physical and technical aspects of the congregation. This means that while there may be special projects and programs for outreach, there needs to be well prayed over and planned out programs for growth which are imparted to, and embraced by, the membership of the congregation. Outreach and growth start in the congregation before anyone goes out the door. Related to growth is the phenomenon of crowds drawing crowds. It may be easier for the larger congregations to grow because they are larger. The smaller a congregation is, the harder it must work to grow. Shishkoff's strategy would certainly help in bringing a congregation to a stage where it can grow more effectively.

Table 45: Number of People Who Have Left the Congregation in the Past Year

Level	#	%
1–5	11	37
6–10	8	27
11–5	5	17
16–20	0	0
20+	1	3

The leaders listed the following reasons for how they perceived people who left their congregation:
- move out of area
- disagree with Messianic vision
- charismatic emphasis
- distance to travel
- backsliding
- death

These reasons suggest that being either charismatic or non-charismatic will make little difference in people leaving a congregation. There are always people who will leave because they differ no matter the emphasis of the congregation. One factor that stands out is the people who left because they did not have a Messianic vision. This indicates that the vision should be taught more clearly to those inquiring about the congregation. Those in the congregation should be reminded of it more frequently so they know why they are there and what the congregation's prime goals are.

Table 46: Leader's Perception of Congregation

Perception	#	%
Growing	23	77
At a Plateau	5	17
Shrinking	2	7

Most congregations are perceived as growing, expressing an optimism about the movement and what God is doing in bringing His people to redemption. Some perceive themselves as at a plateau. This may be because growth is slow in a Messianic congregation owing to its specialized ministry. Those who perceive their congregations as shrinking did so because of recent splits or internal problems.

Table 47: Activities of the Congregation to Foster the Fellowship and Social Life of the Congregation

Activity	**#**	**%**
Worship Services	23	80
Social Gathering	26	87
Outings	17	57
Special Projects	14	47

Other activities indicated include ladies bible studies, prayer meetings, bagel breakfasts, growth groups, pot lucks, Bible studies, and home groups.

The focus of Messianic congregations is more than just evangelism; they seek to build up the congregation in areas of fellowship and practical, as well as spiritual, ministry. If they were merely mission stations in disguise, as anti-missionaries claim, they would not have any fellowship or support ministries.

In conclusion, the results of the survey have shown that some variables in Messianic congregations have little or no bearing on growth and outreach, while others make a significant contribution. From the survey, the data suggests the main elements of Messianic worship are preaching and music. This would suggest that Messianic leaders should seek to be as well trained for their ministries as possible. Congregations should also seek to develop their music ministries because of the character of Messianic worship. Because ten percent of Messianic leaders were raised in a Messianic environment, Messianic believers should seek to place a strong emphasis on education, developing curricula, and encouraging their young people in their Messianic walks.

This study shows that the charismatic factor will not necessarily cause a congregation to gain or lose people. It does not appear to be a main factor of growth.

Messianic congregations should place a greater emphasis on outreach to believing intermarried couples looking for a middle ground in which to worship and be a part, as well as to unsaved intermarried couples.

Jewish cultural elements in worship seem to have little value in outreach, but have value in identity and setting. The facilities in which Messianic congregations meet shows no statistical evidence of affecting the size or growth of the Messianic congregation. While, for the sake of identification and outreach, it may be advisable for a congregation to have its own facility, either owned or leased, this cannot be substantiated by the data gathered in this study.

Most congregations have a good opportunity to grow through the visitors they have. They need to find new ways of attracting and keeping those who visit.

Because of the opportunities of outreach through holiday celebrations, Messianic congregations should orient these services more evangelistically to seize the opportunities for outreach.

It would appear that the factors affecting growth in Messianic congregations are less connected to programs and more to the attitudes of the people in the congregations. However, some variable factors within the Messianic context are valuable for outreach and should be developed as the movement matures.

Messianic congregations have a threefold function. They witness to the Jewish community, build up the body of believers, and maintain and strengthen Jewish identity. They are in a unique position to share the Messiah as insiders, as Jews sharing with Jews. They are also in a unique position to reach out to intermarried couples who are not accepted in the Jewish community and not ministered to effectively in traditional church settings. Messianic congregations will need to focus their energies on those things that help build the congregations: outreach and evangelism. This needs to be activated by training the people in the congregations to expect growth and welcome it.

People need to be encouraged to reach out personally to visitors in the congregation, and to friends and neighbors. Music ministries should be enhanced to aid congregational growth.

This study will certainly not be the last on Messianic Judaism. It is but a picture of one stage in the development of a mighty movement in an early phase. It remains to be seen in what way the Lord will use Messianic Judaism for His glory and towards His goal of humanity's redemption.

Endnotes

[1] Rausch, *Messianic Judaism*, pp.73–78.

APPENDIX TWO

PARTICIPATING CONGREGATIONS IN OPINION SURVEY

Beth Messiah Congregation	East Hanover, New Jersey
Olive Tree Congregation	Plainview, New York
Beth Messiah Congregation	Columbus, Ohio
Beth Ariel Fellowship	Brentwood, California
Kehilat Mashiach	Cincinnati, Ohio
Kehilat Ariel	San Diego, California
Vineyard Congregation	Long Grove, Illinois
Emmanuel Messianic Congregation	Columbia, Maryland
Adat HaTikvah	Chicago, Illinois
Congregation Or Chadash	Clearwater, Florida
Beth Messiah Congregation	Philadelphia, Pennsylvania
Congregation Beth Shalom	Springfield, Massachusetts
Beth Messiah Congregation	Rockville, Maryland
Shema Yisrael Congregation	Rochester, New York
Tree of Life Congregation	San Diego, California
Tikvat Yisrael	Cleveland, Ohio
Beth Messiah Congregation	Cincinnati, Ohio
Beth Yeshua Congregation	Youngstown, Ohio
Adat HaMashiach Congregation	Irvine, California
Beth Israel Congregation	Clearwater, Florida
Seed of Abraham	St. Louis Park, Minnesota
Adat Yeshua	Albuquerque, New Mexico

Beth HaTikvah	St. Louis, Missouri
Congregation Rosh Pina	Baltimore, Maryland
Ohev Yisrael	Springfield, Virginia
Temple Aron Kodesh	Fort Lauderdale, Florida
Congregation Bnai Maccabim	Highland Park, Illinois
Tsemach Adonai	Santa Cruz, California
Ruach Israel	Wellesley, Massachusetts
Beth Jacob Congregation	Jacksonville, Florida

While this is not a complete list of Messianic congregations, it is a representative sample of congregations from all three Messianic groups. It represents those congregations which consented to participate in the survey and met the criteria set forth in the first appendix.

APPENDIX THREE

SURVEY AND ANALYSIS OF JEWISH BELIEVERS ATTENDING CHURCHES

Apart from the many Jewish believers who are part of Messianic congregations, there are many others who worship primarily in churches. Some who do so fault the Messianic Jewish congregations for not having the depth or fullness of programs to appeal to them. Others blame the Jewish missions for steering Jewish believers to churches and by-passing the Messianic congregations. Still others blame the Jewish believers themselves for selling out to the comfort of well established churches with all the programs and activities rather than helping establish the foundation for a strong Messianic Jewish movement for the future.

Seeking to find out why Jewish believers go to churches I conducted a survey in February, 1992 of Jewish believers who worship primarily in churches. The purpose of this survey was to develop a profile of the types of Jewish believers who attend Gentile oriented churches instead of more Jewish oriented congregations. The goal is to better understand what contributes to their choice of present congregational homes.

The answers should be helpful to Messianic congregations in finding out what needs they are not meeting and may be able to meet, and to focus on reaching those Jewish people who would best benefit from a Messianic congregational experience. It should also promote a better understanding of the needs of Jewish believers outside the Messianic congregational movement so that their needs can also be met.

This survey was conducted by telephone interviews with seventy Jewish believers from all geographic locations of the U.S.A., sixty-eight of whom attend churches and not Messianic congregations as their main place of worship. The sampling is not large, but should be sufficient to give a general portrait of Jewish believers in churches. I sought to reach specifically those Jewish believers who identified themselves as Jewish and as primarily church attenders. It would be logistically impossible to poll Jewish believers in churches who no longer identify themselves as Jews, because there would have no way of identifying them as Jewish.

Jewish Background:	%
Traditional	54%
Secular	36%
Jewish Believer	4%
Christian	7%

The above figures reflect the type of Jewish upbringing of the respondents. Most indicated a traditional upbringing, which, for the purpose of this survey refers to any kind of Jewish religious upbringing, from Orthodox or Reform. Most of the respondents who indicated a traditional background mentioned it was Reform Judaism. More than half had some kind of religious upbringing. Those who were from either mixed marriages or are second generation believers indicated Jewish believer or Christian backgrounds.

Age:	%
20's	20%
30's	34%
40's	39%
50's	5%
60+	2%

Agency of Salvation	%
Friends	32%
Church Outreach	18%
Mission Outreach	11%
Messianic Congregations	2%
Spouse/Family	16%
Spiritual Experience	9%
Self Study	13%

Year Became a Believer	%
pre-1960	5%
1960-64	2%
1965-69	4%
1970-74	13%
1975-79	13%
1980-84	18%
1985-89	29%
1990-92	18%

Most of the people polled were in their twenties to forties and became believers in the last twenty years. The principle factors which influenced them to become believers were friends, family, church and mission outreach. The strongest influence apparently was friendship evangelism. A later question indicated that fellowship is one of the most important factors in determining where they would attend services. This could indicate a link between how a person came to Yeshua and where they later fellowship.

Terms of Self-Description	%
Hebrew Christian	5%
Jewish Christian	27%
Messianic Jew	27%
Completed Jew	13%
Jewish Believer	20%
Believer	9%
Jews for Jesus	7%
Jew	2%
Christian	30%
No term	2%

Most Jewish believers in churches seem to favor a term of self-description that identifies them as Jewish as well as being a believer. This indicates the importance of Jewish identity to Jewish believers in churches. The term *Jew* by itself is not sufficient for most Jewish believers in churches perhaps because their identities are also tied to the Messiah. It is also interesting that the single most common term of self-designation was Christian, indicating that Jewish identity is not important for some.

Jewishness is Mainly	%
Religion	7%
Culture	27%
Ethnic Identity	55%
All of the Above	23%

The majority of Jewish believers polled considered Jewishness to be an ethnic identity (who you are), and secondarily, a cultural identity (how you express yourself). Jewishness appears to be regarded as something not rejected when turning to the Messiah. Some have argued that Jewishness is cast aside by Jewish believers in churches, but this is not indicated by their responses. It is still retained, but is apparently expressed differently. It may be this belief that Jewishness is an ethnic identity that contributes to their presence in churches. They may feel their ethnic identity is inherent, and therefore not jeopardized by church membership.

Ways Jewish Believers Maintain Jewish Heritage	%
Celebrate Holidays	48%
Maintain Family Ties	7%
Synagogue Attendance	11%
Fellowship w/JB's	13%
Support Israel	4%
Keep Kosher	2%
None	21%

This question sought to ascertain in what ways Jewish

believers polled maintain their Jewishness. Most maintain their ties through celebration of Jewish holidays and fellowship with other Jewish believers. The most celebrated holy days indicated were Hanukkah and Passover at 16% each. Only 2% celebrated the High Holy Days, Rosh Hashanah and Yom Kippur. Hanukkah may be celebrated because of its proximity to Christmas, and Passover because of its Messianic importance. It is interesting that only 2% celebrate the High Holy Days in contrast to the Messianic Jewish congregational members, who celebrate them at 100%.

Marital Status	%
Single (never been married)	32%
Single (Divorced)	13%
Single (widowed)	0%
Married to Gentile	48%
Married to Unsaved Jew	0%
Married to Jewish Believer	7%

Children	%
Under 12	32%
12-18	18%
18-25	18%
None	45%

The marital factor is also significant. 93% of the Jewish believers in churches are either married to Gentile spouses or are single. This may indicate that Jewishness is not a prime concern in their lives. If it were, they might have married Jewish believers or would be worshiping in places where they would meet potential spouses who are Jewish believers. In several cases, marriage to Gentile spouses was given as the reason they were in churches and not Messianic congregations.

The issue of children is a mixed one. Most people with children talked about the need to pass on their heritage to their children, but expressed frustration about how to accomplish this. Some seemed unsure as to what exactly it was they were trying to pass on or how it was they were supposed to be passing it. The

Messianic congregations present themselves as a means to pass on Jewish heritage to children, so this issue is different for this particular group of Jewish believers. This is an area where both Messianic congregations and Jewish missions might seek to provide resources to Jewish believers in traditional churches. This kind of support may eventually lead to these Jewish believers participating in Messianic congregations, but even if it did not, it would at least support fellow Jewish believers in their desire to hold on to their heritage, and to preserve it in their children.

Present Place of Worship	%
Denominational Church	64%
Charismatic/Pentecostal	23%
Messianic Congregation	6%
Synagogue	2%
Mission	4%
None	6%

Frequency of Worship	%
Weekly	66%
2–3x Week	20%
2–3x Month	6%
Monthly	2%
Rarely	7%

Number of Places Attended	%
1	75%
2	13%
3	7%
None	5%

Prior Places of Worship	%
None	39%
Same kind of Church	27%
Different Kind of Church	21%
Other	11%

Things Liked About Former Fellowship
Music/Liturgy	14%
Teaching	13%
Pastor	11%
Location	2%
Fellowship	13%

The picture presented here is of a primarily faithful type of Jewish believer who attends a place of worship with a high level of commitment to the body. They do not appear to be in attendance by compulsion or because they were talked into being there, but because they honestly derive spiritual benefit from where they attend.

Things Liked About Present Place of Worship
Music/Liturgy	41%
Teaching	46%
Pastor	32%
Fellowship	73%
Outreach Programs	14%
Service Opportunities	9%
Sunday School Programs	4%
Spouse Likes It	4%

Anything Jewish about Present Place of Worship:
No	73%
Sponsor Seders	11%
Other Jewish Believers	7%
Messianic Songs	16%

The prime factors for Jewish believers attending their churches appear to be the quality of the fellowship. It is there that they find encouragement in their walk with the Lord. The quality of the teaching and type of music and liturgy also play major roles. Most of these places offer little or no Jewish elements for the Jewish believers attending.

The issue of fellowship may contain several different factors. It is hard to believe that only the churches provide adequate fellowship, and the Messianic congregations do not. This answer may also include the issue of how the individual believer came to know the Lord. The churches may be the places where they were brought and encouraged as a new believer by the person who led them to the Lord. They may also be made to feel more special in a church than in a Messianic congregation where it is not a special thing to be a Jewish believer.

Aspects of Jewishness Important to Maintain

Identity/Ethnicity	41%
Holidays	39%
Jewish Evangelism	4%
Belief in Messiah	4%
Jewish Causes	9%
Jewish Worship style	4%
Family Ties	4%
Fellowship with JB's	2%

Most respondents considered identity and holidays the most important aspects of Jewishness to maintain, and as recognized earlier, belief in the Messiah is part of that identity.

Preference for Day of the Week for Worship

None	79%
Saturday	7%
Sunday	16%

Factors in Determining Worship Location

Teaching	57%
Jewishness	13%
Pastor	9%
Outreach	5%
Liturgy/Music	20%
Fellowship	46%
Location	5%
Denomination	4%
Sunday School	2%

Have Ever Attended Messianic Congregation
Yes 54%
No 46%

Would Ever Attend (or attend again)
Yes 70%
No 9%
Maybe 21%

As seen earlier, teaching, worship, and fellowship are of prime importance to where these Jewish believers worship. It appears that there is little or no bias against Messianic congregations, and in fact, when questioned, most seemed positive about them and would be open, but their present situation did not hold Messianic congregations as viable options.

Literature Received in the Home
Mission Newsletters 86%
Church Newsletters 27%
Messianic Literature 13%
Christian Magazines 39%

The literature received in the home would indicate a strong mission influence in the views of Jewish believers.

The survey only scratches the surface of these issues, yet it does dispel several misconceptions. First, Jewish believers in churches do not all reject the importance or validity of Messianic congregations and have no real negative views about them. They do not attend Messianic congregations for a variety of reasons, mostly relational. The Messianic congregations should not be seen to be deficient in their ministries because Jewish believers in churches do not attend them.

Second, Jewish believers are not in churches because Jewish missions steer them there. Many are in churches because their friends who cared enough to share also brought them into their fellowships.

Third, Jewish believers in churches still have need for outlets of Jewish expression. This needs to be recognized by Messianic congregations, Jewish missions, and their churches and all should seek to provide as many helps as possible.

APPENDIX FOUR
MESSIANIC TRENDS IN THE 1990'S

Since the surveys located in the Appendix One were administered in 1987, there have been many changes in the Messianic congregational movement. Unlike the surveys conducted in the past, these current assertions are not derived from collected data, but reflect changes the author has noticed over the nine years since the survey was originally administered. Much of the previous data still accurately reflects the Messianic movement of the 90's. Only those areas with significant change will be discussed here.

In Table 16: Day of Main Worship Service, the data reflected that more congregations held services on Friday than on other days, while Saturday was the second most popular day of worship and Sunday was a close third. These figures reflected that most congregations had more than one meeting per weekend.

Since that time, there has been a trend towards Saturday services instead of Friday/Saturday or Friday/Sunday. There are several reasons for this shift. Saturday provides a better opportunity to have an effective *Shabbat* school, because it is not late at night. Second, people are more relaxed on Saturday morning, not having to come straight from work or to rush through dinner. The family is thus able to have a Friday evening *shabbat* dinner at home, and then attend a Saturday morning worship service. An additional factor relates to another table in the appendix, Table 23: Congregations with a Torah. This table indicates that in 1987, approximately one third of all congregations surveyed

171

had Torah scrolls. Since that time, a Messianic congregation with a Torah Scroll has become normative. Today, approximately 75–80% of Messianic congregations have and use Torah scrolls in their worship service. This is not only a reflection of U.S. congregations, but congregations in Canada, South America, and Europe as well. As more congregations began to own Torah scrolls, the more they wanted to use them in their services. Since the time to have a Torah service is Saturday morning, congregations began to move their services to Saturday morning. This shift has been so dramatic that today it is rare to find a Messianic congregation with worship services on Friday or Sunday.

A second shift is reflected in the data recorded in Table 20c: What Percentage of Your Male Congregants Wear *T'fillin* (Phylacteries). At the time of the survey, 83 percent of Messianic leaders said *t'fillin* are never used by their congregants, while 17 percent said they had occasional usage. To be fair, this is harder to measure, since *t'fillin* are never worn on *shabbat*. In the 90's, there has been a great shift in *t'fillin* usage. A *minyan* (quorum of ten Jewish men who meet for prayer) has been maintained at the UMJC conferences since 1991, which averaged about 30–60 in daily attendance. Many men put on *t'fillin* for prayer, and many *t'fillin* are sold at the conferences each year. More and more Messianic leaders are seeking to learn how to wear and use *t'fillin* as well. It can be assumed that at least occasional use of *t'fillin* is on the rise in Messianic circles.

The above-mentioned shifts suggest there is a greater move in the direction of traditional Jewish worship. There are more and more congregations utilizing traditional Jewish prayers in their services. Yet this shift is not "movement-wide." If anything, it reflects the beginnings of a rift within the Messianic movement. While there is a genuine shift towards a more traditional service and practice by some congregations, there is another shift away from Jewish tradition towards a more Christian charismatic service. Those that are moving towards a more charismatic service claim that their way is the most Jewish, because of the presence of the *Ruach ha Kodesh* (Holy Sprit). While people are within their rights to worship God as they please, they do not have the right to call it "Jewish," when in fact it is not.

Traditional Jewish practices provide Messianic congregations with links to the Jewish community, while innovation and deviation from the traditions show our freedom but can place us further apart from that community. Some have said that belief in *Yeshua* breaks us off completely from the Jewish community, so we might as well do what we want anyway. The fact is, these ties are not completely severed; but the further we move away, the fewer the ties we will find with the Jewish community.

These shifts are small, yet dramatic. It remains to been seen where this shift, in either direction, will bring Messianic congregations over the next few years. The Messianic movement worldwide continues to change and grow. Many years ago, the first congregations coming out of mission backgrounds, found it radical to wear *yarmulkes* (skullcaps), and their services were more church-like than Jewish in orientation. As the movement grew and developed, it became more and more Jewish in orientation. These observed shifts are part of the continuing development of the Messianic movement, whose future is yet to be seen.

BIBLIOGRAPHY

Bagatti, Bellarmino. *The Church From the Circumcision.* Jerusalem: Franciscan Printing Press, 1984.

Barth, Markus. *The People of God.* Sheffield: JSNT Press, 1983.

Boyle, Isaac. trans. *The Ecclesiastical History of Eusebius Pamphilus.* Grand Rapids: Guardian Press, 1955.

Brandon, S.G.F. *The Fall of Jerusalem and the Christian Church.* London: SPCK, 1978.

Brown, Colin. ed. *The New International Dictionary of New Testament Theology.* English language edition. Grand Rapids: Zondervan Publishing House, 1980.

Brown, Harold O.J. *Heresies: The Image of Christ in the Mirror of Heresy and Orthodoxy from the Apostles to the Present.* Garden City, New York: Doubleday, 1984.

Brunner, Emil. *The Misunderstanding of the Church.* Translated by Harold Knight. Philadelphia: Westminster Press, 1953.

Burton, Ernest. *The International Critical Commentary, The Epistle to the Galatians.* Edinburgh: T. &T. Clark, 1920.

Cranfield, C.E.B. *A Critical and Exegetical Commentary on The Epistle to the Romans.* Vol.2 Edinburgh: T.& T. Clark, 1979.

Danielou, Jean. *The Theology of Jewish Christianity.* Translated & Edited by John A. Baker. Philadelphia: Westminster Press, 1964.

Flannery, Edward. *The Anguish of the Jews.* New York: Quest, 1965.

Flemming, Bruce. C.E. *Contextualization of Theology.* Pasadena: William Carey Library, 1980.

Fruchtenbaum, Arnold G. *Hebrew Christianity: Its Theology, History, and Philosophy.* San Antonio: Ariel Ministries, 1983.

_____ *Israelology: The Missing Link in Systematic Theology.* Tustin, California: Ariel Ministries, 1989.

Fuller, Daniel P. *Gospel and Law: Contrast or Continuum?* Grand Rapids: Eerdmans Publishing Co., 1982.

Gaebelein, Frank E., ed. *The Expositors Bible Commentary.* Grand Rapids: Zondervan, 1976.

Ginsberg, Louis. ed. *The Legends of the Jews.* Philadelphia: Jewish Publishing Company, 5728 [1968].

Harris, R. Laird; Archer, Gleason L.; and Waltke, Bruce K. eds. *Theological Wordbook of the Old Testament.* Vol. I. Chicago: Moody Press, 1980.

Hertz, Joseph. quoted in Pirke Avoth, Edited by Nathaniel Kravitz, Chicago: Jewish Way Magazine of Chicago, 1951.

Jay, Eric G. *The Church—It's Changing Image Through Twenty Centuries.* Atlanta: John Knox Press, 1978.

Jocz, Jacob. *The Jewish People and Jesus Christ.* Third edition. Grand Rapids: Baker Book House, 1979.

Juster, Daniel C. *Jewish Roots.* Rockville: Davar Publishing, 1986.

Klijn, A.F.J. and Reinink,G.J. *Patristic Evidence for Jewish-Christian Sects.* Leiden: E. J. Brill, 1973.

Kung, Hans. *The Church.* New York: Sheed & Ward, 1967.

Levey, Samson H. "Best Kept Secret of the Rabbinic Tradition." *Judaism* 21, Fall 1972.

Longenecker, Richard N. *The Christology of Early Jewish Christianity.* London: SCM Press 1970; reprint ed., Grand Rapids: Baker Book House, 1981.

McComiskey, Thomas E. *The Covenants of Promise.* Grand Rapids: Baker Book House, 1985.

Milgrom, Jacob. *The JPS Torah Commentary: Numbers.* Philadelphia: The Jewish Publication Society, 5750/1990.

Morris, Leon. *New Testament Theology.* Grand Rapids: Academie/ Zondervan Books, 1986.

Palliere, A. *The Unknown Sanctuary.* New York: Block, 1928.

Pritz, Ray A. *Nazarene Jewish Christianity: From the New Testament Period Until Its Disappearance in the Fourth Century.* Leiden: E.J. Brill, 1988.

Rausch, David A. *Messianic Judaism: Its History, Theology, and Polity.* New York: Edwin Mellen Press, 1982.

_____ *A Legacy of Hatred. Why Christians Must Not Forget the Holocaust.* Chicago: Moody Press, 1984.

Roberts, Alexander, and Donaldson, James, eds. *The Anti-Nicene Fathers.* 10 Vols.(Grand Rapids: Eerdmans reprint 1981). Coxe, A. Cleveland. Editor. Vol. 5. Fathers of the Third Century.

Saucy, Robert L. *The Church in God's Program.* Chicago: Moody Press, 1972.

Schonfield, Hugh J. *The History of Jewish Christianity.* London: Duckworth, 1936.

Schwartz-Bart, Andre. *The Last of the Just.* New York: Atheneum Publishers, 1960.

Silberman, Charles E. *A Certain People: American Jews and Their Lives Today.* New York: Summit, 1985.

Simon, Marcel. *Jewish Sects at the Time of Jesus.* Translated by James H. Farley. Philadelphia: Fortress Press, 1967.

Stern, David H. *Messianic Jewish Manifesto.* Jerusalem Jewish New Testament Publications, 1988.

Thompson, A.E. *A Century of Jewish Missions,* New York: H. Revell Fleming Company, 1902.

Unpublished Materials

Constitution of the Fellowship of Messianic Congregations